YOUR LIFE YOUR WAY

A PRACTICAL GUIDE TO GETTING YOUR S**T TOGETHER

PAULA MEIR

Contents

Dedication

To those people who have crossed my path for a reason and to my husband and boys who constantly give me the courage to be the best that I can be. Thank you.

About the Author

Paula Meir has over 20 years of experience dealing with people's problems. As an accomplished HR consultant, Qualified Executive Coach and NLP Master Practitioner, she has seen most things and doesn't get surprised by any of it. She has been a divorcee, a single parent and, at some point, has suffered with nearly every issue in this book. She is married to a highly functioning and creative husband, has two independent, handsome sons and a musical stepson. A Springer Spaniel called Rocky and a Springerdoodle called Coco Chanel complete her blended family.

Preface, My Personal Context

I originally started writing this book with no intention of sharing this information. Not because I was trying to hide it (although very few people in my life know about it), but rather because I just didn't think it was relevant. Why would you – the reader – care? Only when I started to write the book did it become clear that I needed to add some sort of context.

Most of us live our lives never knowing what's around the corner. I lived most of my life thinking I did.

My mother died from complications caused by Huntington's disease. Looking back and filling in the gaps, it's clear she was showing symptoms of the disease just after I was born. There was a big age gap between me and my siblings. In the early 70s no one talked about Huntington's disease; no one knew what it was and it certainly wasn't a storyline in soap operas! Huntington's disease affects the central nervous system and that damage gets progressively worse over time, resulting in changes to coordination, movement, cognition and behaviour. It is a hereditary condition with no cure, and on average people die 15 years after first exhibiting symptoms. And being a hereditary disease means there is a 50/50 chance I have inherited the faulty gene that causes Huntingdons.

Unfortunately, when so little was known about the disease, the symptoms were often attributed to something else, including alcohol abuse. Ironically, my Mum, no doubt confused and scared by her own physical deterioration, eventually did turn to alcohol. When I was in my early teens she was sectioned and sent to an institution – a cruel and unusual punishment for having a disorder the doctors simply didn't understand. It goes without saying that these traumatic events shaped my life, but that's not really the reason I'm telling you.

That 50/50 chance of inheriting the condition, really impacts how you view the world and how you live your life. It's like living life every day on the flip of a coin – believing you're normal like everyone else, and then remembering you're not. Some families are lucky and none of the children are affected. In some families all the children are affected and in others only some. But it's a cruel disease either way. Those who don't have the condition often feel "survivor guilt" at being the one who was spared! In our family, my brother also died of complications from the disease.

Not knowing whether I had Huntington's or not has had a *profound* impact on my life. It influenced EVERY major decision I made – certainly in my twenties and thirties. In many ways, it was the canvas on which I painted the rest of my life. Only for me, that life was likely to be over by the time I was 40. But I refused to let the uncertainty define who I was or rob me of experiences I felt passionate about. It did, however, accelerate the timetable…

I didn't go to university. Instead I got married and had children. Huntington's tends to show up around the age it showed up in the parent. In my case that would be late 30s, early 40s. I always knew I wanted a family, but I didn't want my children to suffer the way I had as a child, having to watch my mother deteriorate mentally and physically. Having my family early meant that they would be into adulthood before I ever showed any signs of the disease – assuming I had it. Obviously, the possibility of potentially passing on the condition to my children haunted me, but not having a family and then discovering I didn't have it also haunted me. It was an impossible position. Thankfully, my Dad was always very encouraging and was sure that even if the worst happened, science would have found a cure by then. Unfortunately, no cure has been found, so far, although a lot of progress has been made.

Thinking I may have an incurable hereditary disease has been a burden that I have carried most of my life. Every time I've stumbled or momentarily forgot a word or couldn't think of a particular memory, I've panicked. *Is this the beginning?* You might think, "Why don't you get tested?" For most of my life there *was* no test. Then, when one was developed, I couldn't take it. Ironically, although living with the uncertainty of the condition has been incredibly challenging it was preferable to a definitive answer! If I got the "all clear" it would be wonderful. But what if I am tested and don't get the all clear? I would effectively be handed a death sentence.

Instead I chose life – in all its messy, unpredictable glory. I chose to expect the best, but made provisions for the worst. I worked hard to climb the corporate ladder without a university education and made it all the way to the C-suite of global companies, spurred on by a drive to make enough money so that I could manage if I did develop the condition. I have two gorgeous sons who are living life to the full. Perhaps unsurprisingly, my early marriage didn't last, but I have since remarried the love of my life. In order to come to terms with my situation and work with it constructively I've immersed myself in psychology, personal development, and I'm a master practitioner of Neuro Linguistic Programming (NLP).

Today, I use that knowledge to coach others through difficult challenges and it's work I genuinely love.

Not everyone has to deal with the 50/50 chance of a hereditary condition such as Huntington's, but we all have challenges and hurdles to jump. Too many of us allow those challenges to define who we are and what we are capable of, or deserve.

And that's one of the reasons I'm writing this book.

Many of my past experiences have turned me into the person I am today and I have no doubt that I couldn't have done my job of coaching people and sorting out people's problems for 20 years if I hadn't been through what I've been through. Although strange, I am grateful for it. What I've come to understand is that it really doesn't matter what events, situations or circumstances we find ourselves in. What matters is what choices and decisions we make around those things that can positively or negatively impact our future. Do we let those curve balls define us and limit who we are? Or do we press on regardless, go "all in" and meet life with courage and an open heart? Do we use the conditions and circumstances of our life as a crutch or a spring board? Nothing is bad or good – until we make it so. Of course, there are always tough times, but knowing how to manage those times and how to get through the immediate battles can make a huge difference. This book is therefore a collection of tips and techniques that I have used to help me navigate choppy waters. I have also used them to help others and my hope is that they can do the same for you, whatever challenges you face. Remember, each day is a new day. All the experiences we face as we journey through life, all the roads we take, simply move us closer to our destiny. Or they can screw us up as we refuse to change course.

The choice really is ours and ours alone.

Introduction

Yesterday is history, tomorrow is a mystery,
today is a gift of God, which is why we call it the present.

–Bill Keane

If I asked you to describe yourself right now, what would you say? If you met someone you hadn't seen since school and they asked you about yourself and your life, how would you answer? What details would you share? What would you keep to yourself? What events from the past decade or two most readily spring to mind as a quick-fire insight into what you've been up to? What picture would you try to paint? Would you embellish for effect or give an honest snapshot of your life?

I remember watching a TV drama where a detective was standing over a grave, talking to his sergeant about how a whole life can so easily be reduced to a few sentences on a grave stone: "A novel reduced to a Haiku." What a great line.

Each of us have our own story – a rich and deep exploration of our life so far. The problem is, the location and substance of those stories can't always be trusted. It's not that we deliberately fudge the truth (although sometimes we do), it's simply that our experience of our own life is uniquely personal and depends almost entirely on what we make those experiences mean. The meaning itself depends on myriad factors from our early conditioning, to the other important people in our life, to our emotional state at the time, to what other stuff is going on in our life, to who else was involved in the situation etc. These meanings or interpretations of events can very easily turn into "truth". We then search, almost unwittingly, for further evidence of that truth which, of course, we find, further solidifying an idea or opinion of ourselves, or someone else, that has very little basis in fact. But that doesn't matter because it's now part of our personal belief system or individual mythology that goes on to influence what we do, what we think, and how we feel about ourselves, others and the world around us.

Human beings are meaning makers. And it is the meaning we ascribe to situations and events in our life that determines "where" we live and ultimately how happy or unhappy we are. Where we live, as it turns out, is incredibly important. And I don't mean the physical location – those in New York may or may not be happier than those in New Delhi. The location I'm referring to is the past, the present or the future.

Although I was never consciously aware of this phenomenon, and I certainly couldn't have articulated it to you at the time, looking back on my own life I can see the power of this idea in practice. As I mentioned in the preface, my early life was dominated by my mum's illness and then later the uncertainty of not knowing whether I would inherit her condition or not. My method of coping was simple: I stayed in the now (Figure 0.1). I realised, probably by chance, that I couldn't control the past or the future – all I had was this moment. And although it may sound a little *Wuthering Heights* – all dramatic and melancholy – in reality it liberated me to just get on with my life, one day at a time.

Figure 0.1: Rabbit Holes that Distract Us from Now

We are each at the centre of our own universe. Right now, at this moment, there is you, right here (wherever here is for you) reading these words. In life, there is only three locations that matter:

- The past
- The present (Now!)
- The future

And only one of those "locations" is actually real – now!

Living in the *now* is a much less stressful place to be. Operating from the present and seeking to constantly pull ourselves back to the present gives us power, awareness, energy and clarity. It is much easier to access our very best in the present, because we gain access to our 'higher self' in this space. Prophecies of accessing our "higher selves" may seem farfetched, or little more than new age, airy-fairy nonsense, but it's actually logical and biological. Right here, right now is the only moment we have complete control over in any given moment of any given day – regardless of the ups and downs that are occurring in our life. And those moments are hugely influenced by our interior biology and what we chose to focus on.

For most of us, the past consists of re-living or identifying ourselves with negative things or experiences, such as, "I failed at that before, so I'm not going to try it again" or "I made such a mess of that; if only I'd said…" or "If it wasn't for [insert name of person we blame] none of this would have happened…" Too often, the past is a super-highway to negative experiences, memories or interpretations that can easily trigger challenging emotions such as guilt, regret, anger, blame or sadness.

But, we can't change the past, so constantly looping into re-runs of old conversations or experiences is actually a form of self-harm. It's also a pointless waste of time. So what if you've finally thought of the perfect come back to an argument with your partner 3 months after the divorce! The moment has gone. Reliving the conversation and getting to say your killer line in front of the mirror, or in your imagination, won't alter the reality of the original conversation.

The past's power lies in its ability to teach us. The past allows us to fine tune the way we behave and connect the dots, so we don't keep repeating the same lesson over and over again. It helps us avoid situations we want to avoid in the future or find better ways of handling tricky situations. The past helps us to develop the mental and emotional resilience we need to embrace the present and create a meaningful future. It allows us to shine some much-needed light on the negative patterns and unhelpful conditioning that can often keep us trapped in negative thinking and negative habits. That's its only purpose. As the adage goes, if we don't learn from the past we are destined to repeat it.

The future, on the other hand, is equally mercurial. For most of us, the future consists of fantasies, assumptions, hopes or fears around what "might" happen or what could happen if such and such a person just does X – tying ourselves in knots trying to predict the unpredictable. At least when we get lost in reverie about the past we are thinking about what actually happened (although our interpretation of those events can be wildly inaccurate). In the future, everything we come up with is a fantasy or illusion created by our imagination, based on little or no evidence! And yet, those stories create fast-track access to a whole raft of usually negative emotional states, such as anxiety, worry, uncertainty or fear. It's amazing how brilliantly we are able to manufacture a future that fits snugly around our fears and insecurities – all because we like to be proven right, so we can say, "See, my life sucks – I told you so!" Perversely, we feel comforted by our ability to predict a negative outcome before it's even happened. At least that way we get to learn how to live with the disappointment or failure, right? In my mind, I was pretty convinced I had the Huntington's gene. That outcome fit snugly around my darkest fear and deepest insecurities and allowed me to prepare myself, rather than be surprised by it later on. Thankfully, my preparation involved cramming as much into the early part of my life as I could, but it could so easily have gone the other way!

Clearly, our present influences our future and the choices we make in each moment will impact that future – positively or negatively. But, jumping forward in time into some fantasy re-creation of what life might be like, or how a situation could play out, is not always helpful. It can be extremely helpful in preparing for certain situations. For example, jumping into a future interview and imagining all the questions you might be asked can be useful in helping you prepare. But living there is as pointless and futile as living in the past.

This is the nature of the human condition. We may see each other going about our day, but inside most of us are not operating authentically "in the moment". We are either living in the past or hypothesising about the future. We look like we are interacting with each other, but each of us is presenting a visible avatar that is "interacting" on autopilot, while the real us is stewing over some past event or possible future scenario!

It's ironic, but as human beings we have two contradictory tendencies. When there isn't that much going on in our lives in the present, or when there is too much going on, we tend to disappear into the future or the past. It is here that we get to make up stories.

Quiet often, when those stories are negative, we look to these places in order to justify our feelings about something or someone or ourselves. Worse still, we can very easily build false identifies about who we are from these stories and pull the past or potential future onto our present (or now). These stories can keep us stuck in limiting or destructive situations, or make us fearful of pursuing what we really want to do. Something called "confirmation bias" invades our brain and pollutes our thinking. Confirmation bias, also known as "myside bias" is the tendency to search for, interpret, favour, and recall information in a way that confirms our pre-existing beliefs or hypotheses, while giving disproportionately less consideration to alternative possibilities. In other words, we look for and find "evidence" that supports what we already believe to be true about ourselves, others, events etc. and will frequently dismiss or ignore contrary "evidence" that negates or refutes that initial perception or belief.

This negative storytelling from the past or future also has a physical impact on our bodies and brains, because it changes the physiological make-up of our internal system. This is an incredibly impressive party trick if you stop and think about it… We are able to conjure up an image of something that either did or didn't happen and turn on emotional responses to this figment of our imagination. So, we get to feel something very real, usually negative, in the present based on what we created from our imagination about the future or the past. I am sure you know at least one person in your life who is *very* good at this.

Author Dr Richard Moss believes that when we habitually leave or abandon the present we are postponing a direct relationship with reality (and our feelings and emotions in the moment) and in doing so we distance ourselves from our true selves and lose awareness of "now". Quite often this can happen because we want to avoid the emotional content of the present moment, especially when it's tough. However, to deny or avoid feelings as they arise only leads to a "storing up" of those feelings. Often we talk of "bottling up our emotions". This is exactly this process. The problem, as anyone who has tried this approach will tell you, is it doesn't work forever. Sooner or later the bottle gets full and those emotions leak out somewhere. Sometimes the result is explosive, sometimes it's a quiet oozing of emotional residue. Both are toxic and have a profound impact on our mental and physical health.

Acknowledging and allowing yourself to feel and identify with an emotion in the present is the only way of reducing it or moving through it completely, and this book is your guide to how to do that.

It is designed to help you to get back to *right here, right now* – regardless of the challenges you are facing. Whether you feel stuck, constantly in the middle of a drama, living a mediocre life, or are struggling with strong emotions, going through a break-up or facing tough choices... When we are able to use the past constructively to make better choices in the present and positively influence our future then it is helpful. Spending too much time there, reliving past mistakes or dissecting past conversations, is not.

Similarly, taking time to think about what you want to achieve and where you want your life to take you is a sensible and smart approach, but disappearing into endless fantasy scenarios without getting into action and making decisions today that support those dreams is equally futile. Use the future as a way to road test your dreams and work backwards to figure out what you need to do in order to make it a reality. But beyond that, stay present.

When we come back to the moment and live each one as it arises – life is just easier. I'm not saying we are always going to sail through our challenges, but when we stay with those issues and the tough emotions they can stir up, and lean into them, they are rarely as bad as the stories we create from the past or future that keep us stuck, afraid and unhappy. Although I didn't fully appreciate it at the time, this was my strategy for coping with my mum's illness and the fear that I could end up inheriting her condition. In doing so, I liberated myself and just got on with my life. And you can do the same.

If something in your life isn't working, or you are aware of changes you need to make, don't be the person who waits for something to break, or something to improve as if by magic. Don't be the person who waits for someone else to change or someone else to see the error of *their* ways. Don't be the person who tolerates the drama and angst in their life for an "easy life". There is nothing "easy" about that life – and you know it! Maintaining the status quo, putting on a brave face, smiling for the camera when you really want to weep, is no way to live – it is robbing you of the love, joy, accomplishment and happiness you deserve. If something in your life isn't working – it's time for action.

Getting our own sh**t together isn't just something we all need to do for ourselves, it allows us to help and support others to do the same. I have lost count of the people I've come across in my life who are brimming with talent and ability, but who constantly thwart that potential by getting in their own way and the way of others – simply because they've not got their s**t together. All the luck, ability, talent, opportunity or advantage in the world can so easily come to nothing if we don't learn how to get a handle on our emotions, develop our cognitive and emotional intelligence, and foster our mental resilience to deal constructively with the inevitable highs and lows of life. It's time to unleash your potential, whatever that looks like for you.

Be open, be honest, with yourself and others. And remember – Fortune Favours the Brave...

Chapter 1
Reality Check

The definition of insanity is doing the same thing over and over again expecting different results.

–Albert Einstein

Are you unhappy in your job, with your health, or in your relationship, but can't seem to be able to muster the energy to do anything about it? Are you wanting to make a change but don't know how or where to start? Does the prospect of change excite you and terrify you in equal measure? Do people ask you how you are only to hear yourself say, "Fine", knowing that you're really not fine at all? Do you feel like you are presenting a front to the world that really isn't your reality? Are you lying to yourself about how happy you are? Are you sick of hearing yourself complain about the same situations over and over again? Or perhaps you are in that awkward limbo stage, where things are not really bad enough to leave, but they are not good enough to stay either. If so, you may be stuck.

Feeling stuck is uncomfortable and frustrating. It robs us of joy and huge amounts of energy. It is also incredibly stressful – even though we may not realise it at the time because we get so used to being stuck. When we are stuck in a terrible job, bad relationship, toxic friendship or challenging financial situation, we can often feel powerless to make a change. We tell ourselves, "Oh, it's not that bad" or "If I just hang in there it will get better." We gravitate to others in our lives who are in a poor situation to help us validate our indecision, or worse, we decide to act as the sacrificial lamb: "I will endure being unhappy because of my [children], my [financial state] or [.........] – just fill in the gap to suit; you can use most things. A number of these "reasons" may even be valid, but in my experience children actually want their parents to be happy and financial situations can change, so be sure to really consider the merit of your argument before sacrificing your happiness.

Occasionally, we can be rocked by some sort of crisis which forces our hand and brings about the change we so desperately need. In many ways, being in crisis is easier than being stuck because change is often forced upon us – whether we are ready for it or not. Unfortunately, feeling stuck rarely feels like a crisis. It's not usually accompanied by extreme, intense pain. Instead it's like toothache – a relentless, gradual discomfort that grinds us down over time.

We start out as young adults dreaming about what our life should look like: where we'll live and work, who we will marry, the type of house we will live in, the holidays we'll enjoy, how many children we will have, etc. Many of us like to map out our lives and will do so according to our values, beliefs, culture, upbringing and circumstances. Of course, life rarely goes to plan for any of us. This lack of alignment between where we thought we'd be or how we thought our life would turn out can be destabilising and discombobulating. It can also challenge the identity we hold for ourselves – we are not who we thought we were – and this disconnect begins to create tension or a vacuum which can feel very uncomfortable. In the course of everyday life, it's incredibly easy to become defined by titles and labels. We become "wife", "husband", "executive", "artist", "mother", "father" etc. But when our expectations of that experience don't match the reality, or we are unsatisfied or frustrated by the reality, then we question who we really are. If I am not *that* then who am I? This is especially scary when we have identified with that label for a long time. For example, it's the cause of "empty-nest syndrome" when parents, especially mothers, struggle to come to terms with their place in the world once the children have left home.

Being stuck can create unhealthy dependency: I need my job because, *who am I without it?* I need my husband/wife because, *who am I without them?* Anything that threatens that status quo, even if we feel change is necessary, can feel as though we are about to spontaneously combust! This can be a major factor in decreasing our own independence and confidence which, of course, exacerbates our sense of being stuck. We know something has to change, but we are terrified of the void that change may bring, so we ignore it or distract ourselves instead.

We take on more work and immerse ourselves in "busy" so we don't have time to think about it. Or, we seek out a reward or outlet for putting up with the situation such as smoking, drinking too much or having an affair. Of course, these "solutions" don't work long term. They may provide a welcome distraction, but in the end, they simply bring a new set of problems.

We may choose just to accept the situation, telling ourselves, "Oh, well, I've made my bed now I've got to lie in it" – as though we have some sort of moral obligation to live with wrong choices forever and be constantly reminded of our mistakes. What an absurd idea! Everyone makes mistakes or finds themselves in situations that no longer work. Staying in that situation or doing nothing to improve it is what's really absurd. This approach may even feel like the easiest solution, but it can have a massive negative impact on our confidence, self-esteem and enjoyment of life. I've seen brilliant and talented people systematically taken apart by a toxic work environment, their job, or an unhappy relationship. And, it can go on for years.

If your situation turns you into someone you don't recognise or someone you don't want to be, pay attention to that. As human beings, we are naturally hopeful, but when we are stuck in a bad situation our inherent hopefulness can be our worst enemy. We "hope" that we can change someone, or we can change a situation, or, worst of all, we hope it will change all by itself if we just wait long enough! Guess what? It won't change until you change it. Use that realisation to fuel your first step toward change.

The First Step Toward Change

If you recognise that you are currently stuck in a situation – whether that is a relationship you no longer want to be in, a job you no longer enjoy, or some other situation that is sapping your energy and enthusiasm for life – then it's time to take stock and be honest with yourself.

> *The truth will set you free,*
> *but first it will piss you off.*
>
> **–Joe Klaas**

A huge part of the "stuckness" we experience is caused by our unwillingness to face our own truth. We know this truth: it is the thoughts that emerge in the silence, the feelings we recognise as real in the small hours of the morning, but push away when the sun emerges once again. As the quote above reminds us, it's not always easy and we may not always enjoy the process, but the reward is freedom and that is always worth pursuing.

The stuckness we experience is also exacerbated by our propensity for binary, "all-or-nothing", thinking. We worry about life "on the other side". The fear of doing anything overwhelms our motivation of doing anything, so we oscillate between what I call "two places of doom": if I stay it's going to be awful; if I leave it's going to be painful. When presented with these imaginary choices (remember, they are just stories based on the past or extrapolated into the future) it's easy to decide it's just not worth the hassle! I promise you, *it is*. Life is short. How much more of it are you going to waste before it's too late?

One of the reasons we don't move to action is because we tend to imagine only two outcomes – either leave or stay – and both have negative consequences. We rarely stop to consider the myriad choices in between. Part of this is down to evolutionary biology. When we are unhappy or stressed our brain goes into emergency fight, flight or freeze mode and gets stuck there (more on that in Chapter 5). This reduces our ability to think clearly or creatively, which would allow us to problem-solve more effectively. We also sometimes resist moving to action because we genuinely don't know how to solve something. We either overcomplicate the situation or get so used to it that the stuckness feels normal (it's not normal it's just habit). Either way, we struggle even to envisage what "different" might look like and how that might feel.

It's interesting to understand how habit loops work. In his book *Power of Habit*, author Charles Duhigg writes about how the brain creates a habit (Figure 1.1)

Figure 1.1: How Habits are Formed

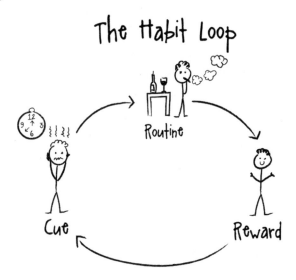

A cue, or trigger, triggers the routine or automatic action (physical/mental/emotional) which delivers the reward. This is where our brain decides whether this particular loop is worth remembering. We may not be able to change the cue, trigger or reward, but we can change the routine which in turn changes the habit.

This means that our habits are what we choose them to be! Once we recognise this and choose the change it is automatic.

It's time to really examine those habits and consider the continuum of options you may have to help you make positive change. Just because you are stuck at the moment doesn't mean that you will always be stuck. There may be ways that you could change your situation or make some small adjustments that would make a huge difference to how you feel. Apart from

31

raising the stakes and stress level, the "all-or-nothing", "stay or go" binary approach is not always the best solution.

The first step, therefore, is to get really honest with yourself about what's going on. Take some time out, go for a walk in nature, by yourself, and consider the following questions...

- Is there any part of you that wants to save this situation? Every situation, even a bad one, has advantages. Recognise and identify what the advantages and disadvantages are, so that you have the clearest, most realistic picture of the situation.
- With everything that you know and have experienced so far about the situation, everything you've heard and seen, is there really going to be any change? If it's possible, how long are you willing to wait?
- If you are choosing to stay in that situation and be more creative with options, be clear about what you need and would like. Where are the boundaries drawn (do they need to be redrawn?) and what will and won't you tolerate?
- Is there a point to what you are doing (or not doing)? Is there an outcome or end game that could make persevering worth the effort in the long run?
- Are you happy with the status quo?
- Are you being who you truly are and want to be whilst "stuck" in this situation?
- Are you in control? If you aren't in control, start taking some back. Even if you decide to stay in the situation, long or short term, realise that you are choosing to do that. Use that choice to fuel additional choices and decisions about how you feel about the situation and what you are going to do. You don't have to go from zero to hero on the stuck-o-meter. Slow and steady often wins the race.

When we run these types of questions through our mind/body system we are better able to access our gut feelings and intuition. We can get away from the brain chatter and justification and feel the truth in our body. When we arrive at the truth for us, it is almost always accompanied by a physical resonance that we feel in our gut or heart. It is never experienced in our head!

For example, as mentioned in the preface, I got married when I was 18 years old. Although we were married for 15 years, I probably spent the last five years deciding how I was going to call an end to the relationship. I created umpteen scenarios, justifications and plans in my mind over those years, but it was only when my youngest son nearly drowned and my husband didn't jump into action that I finally acted on it. I'd reached my "breaking point". It was a whole body, visceral experience that triggered the change.

The first step is to get clear on the situation. Figure out if you want to save the situation and what you are prepared to do to improve it. There is no point hoping and waiting for some miracle intervention that will solve your problem without any effort. Instead, focus on what *you* can do to make things better. If you do want to save the situation, or at least try, then your next step may be to engage a counsellor or executive coach to help you navigate the process. You may not need to "throw the baby out with the bathwater" and instead, a few tweaks and shifts, a refocusing of your end goals or some changes in other areas of your life may be all that's needed to help you to become unstuck.

If, like me, you realise you've reached a point of no return then you need to take action.

⚠

Beware excuses! Get ready for all your well-worn and familiar reasons and justifications to emerge. Change of any type often initiates an internal battle. Think of this like the devil and angel on your shoulders. Although it's never as simple as a good/bad dichotomy, think instead of these two characters as "Quo" (advocating the status quo) and "Go" (advocating change). Quo is going to try and discourage you from facing your reality, so you can carry on doing what you are doing. If you stop for just a minute and really rigour where you are, you might just admit it's not working. Quo knows that if that happens you might just have to do something about it, so you are going to be reminded of every reason, excuse and justification for the status quo possible. Expect it, it's coming. Quo's objective is to "keep you safe" in the familiar, even if the familiar sucks. Quo wants to prevent you from taking the harder road, including rubbishing things you are reading here! Remember confirmation bias: "This is nonsense. Paula doesn't appreciate my unique situation. It's different ... it's not so easy for me to just do it. Besides it's not that bad is it ... blah, blah, blah…" Actively engage "Go" in the dialogue. For every excuse designed to keep you stuck, your job is to come up with two reasons why taking action and making change in your life is going to be beneficial. Get creative if you have to!

Tips and Strategies

The will to believe is the most important
ingredient in creating a belief in change.

–William James

People change their life journeys all the time. There is no reason why you can't be one of them. Believe in yourself. If you've been honest with yourself and know in your heart that you need to get yourself unstuck and back in the flow of life, then the next step is to look at your own personal narrative as it relates to your situation. This is your story or thought habit.

Most of our personal narratives or stories are not necessarily based on fact, but instead represent what we recall of a situation or the PR spin we put on our experiences to justify inertia to ourselves and others. Often they are the stories we use to help us cope with the status quo. Examples may include: I'm unhappy in my relationship, but I know he/she loves me, or I hate my job, but I'm hoping to get that promotion which will make it all worthwhile.

It's amazing what we can tell ourselves in order to make a bad situation seem acceptable. In most cases, the first part of the story is true and the second part is justification for the first! If you are in this situation, or know someone who is, one of the most common things you will hear is, "I can't believe I didn't do it or recognise it sooner." A good example of this was when I was in my last job, working many hours, and being in a constant state of stress. I was physically and mentally on high alert all the time. I had worked hard to get to where I was. I had a team that needed me, and a number of other people who I worked with and coached to help them through their day too. I knew deep down that the situation wasn't going to improve, but ever-hopeful I ploughed on getting increasingly stressed. I started to lose confidence and got more emotional as the days, weeks and months went by. For months, I knew I wanted to leave but told myself, "But, I get paid well and I'm the main breadwinner so I can't leave … It's not that bad, I get to help people … I can't leave, I'm good at my job…" and the old chestnut, "It will get better…" I tried to convince myself that it would somehow turn around and people would start to recognise my contribution, so it would all be OK.

We know when we are lying to ourselves. It's best just to accept it and take action.

Take Control

You may be thinking, "Well that's all very well to say, but the reason I'm stuck is that I can't take control!" Again, this is usually a result of "all-or-nothing" thinking, or a dominant partner/situation. You don't have to change everything overnight. Instead, admit where you are right now and decide where you want to get to. Make a plan and start making some different choices. Small steps are better than no steps at all.

Concentrate on the things you can change (i.e. you) and stop trying to change the things you can't (organisation or partner). Remember the serenity prayer…

Grant me the serenity to accept the things I cannot change,
Courage to change the things I can,
And wisdom to know the difference.

Most of us spend far too much time and energy trying to change what we can't change and complaining bitterly about it. This can, however, start to define who we are and we get comfortable with it. Instead, identify what you can do and move your attention and effort to making those alterations and you will be surprised at how quickly you can become unstuck.

Say, for example, John doesn't like his job. He complains about it so much that his friends outside work forbid him from talking about it! John's looked for something else, but there is nothing locally and he doesn't want to commute too far, because he has a young family and likes being home for dinner. This insight is a bit of a revelation, because John hadn't actually acknowledged what was good about the role. He starts to really think about his job and what he hates about it. The stand-out issues are that he has to prepare and deliver monthly presentations to his team and he dreads it. He also hates his work area because it's nowhere near natural light and he doesn't like the person he sits next to, because they bitch about everything all day long. He doesn't mind his boss. She's not very inspiring though and he's not sure if there is a clear progression path for him or anyone else.

Thinking more constructively about the issue, John realises that he's spent all his energy complaining about the job, rather than getting clearer about what he has control over and what he doesn't have control over. He looks online and finds a local Toastmasters club that are running presentation skills training. He also notices that one of his colleagues who sits in a spot next to the window always comes into work and immediately closes the blinds. As John is making a coffee in the kitchen, that colleague comes in and he asks why they do that. It turns out they are sensitive to the light and prefer working with the blinds drawn. John explains that he would love a little natural light and suggests they swap workstations. The other person agrees and John says he will run it by the boss, just to make sure it's OK. John goes to visit his boss and she tells him she has no objections. At the same time, John takes the opportunity to explain about the Toastmasters course and asks whether the business would pay for it. John's boss is immediately impressed, because she's also aware that he is struggling in that area. Knowing that John is also aware and is proactively trying to solve the problem is encouraging, and this puts John on the promotion radar for the first time. Just by thinking constructively about the situation, instead of applying blanket negativity to it, John focused on what he could change and took action to make those alterations. Relatively easily, John was able to improve his situation and become unstuck. He got better at presentations. He moved workstation and enjoyed more natural light and a nicer view, whilst helping a colleague. And he got away from the person he didn't like without causing a scene!

Of course, not every situation is as straightforward, but there are always things that we can improve or change. Seeing as they are the only things we really have domain over anyway, it's critical that we separate out what we *can* and *can't* change and focus on the former.

Once you are committed to change, draw comfort from the fact that your current situation is no longer permanent – it is simply a temporary state that you will soon be free from. This realisation and re-framing of your current situation can free up your thinking and alleviate some of the accumulated pressure. It can also help to open up your mind to new creative possibilities that you may not have considered before.

Also, stop complaining about the situation to yourself and others. Stop blaming others and stop berating yourself for your lack of action or control up to this point. Instead, use that energy to accept that you are where you are, focus on your new reality and make it happen. Again, pull yourself back from the present. If your "now" is challenging, find refuge in imagining the positive future you are heading toward. But, be sure to action that future in the present, otherwise it's pointless.

Create a New Story

Revisit your current personal narrative and create a new story. Using the examples above, "I'm unhappy in my relationship but I know he/she loves me" could change to "I'm unhappy in my relationship, but I know that once we go our separate ways we will both be happier in the long run." Often what we fail to appreciate in relationships is that both parties deserve to experience reciprocated love. Staying in a relationship when the love is gone not only deprives you of the opportunity for happiness, it also deprives your partner of being with someone who loves them back.

Instead of, "I hate my job, but I'm hoping to get that promotion which will make it all worthwhile" consider creating a new story such as, "I hate my job, but I'm actively focused on finding a better role."

Start imagining what your ideal new situation will look like. Be big and bold. Let your imagination run wild. Have fun with this process. Do you see yourself in a new relationship or do you see yourself enjoying some "single" time in your own apartment? If you want a new relationship, what qualities should your new partner have? What qualities are you going to bring to that partnership? If you want a new job, what type of role do you want? What does it pay? What sort of company is it and what are your colleagues like? Imagine yourself speaking with a new boss you really like. Add as much colour and detail as possible and feel what you will feel when you've made the change and this is your new reality. Imagine stepping into your own shoes a month from now, or two months from now, and feel the euphoria and strength you feel, having made the changes. Create something exciting and motivating outside of your current situation to draw you forward and encourage you to take the daily action you need to reach that new destination.

Consider Your Language

Think about the language you use and make sure it's switched to positive statements. Some examples would be replacing:

- "I can't" with "I will"
- "It's too hard" with "I can create and choose my own future"
- "I don't have any confidence" with "I have been confident in the past and I will use that resource to help me through now"
- "What else will I do?" with "There is opportunity waiting for me"
- "I will be on my own/I won't know what do to" with "I'm independent, capable and excited about the future"
- "There isn't much I can do about it" with "I am in control; I can make choices and choose my reaction and actions"

The wording that you use to think and talk about your situation is very important and impacts the way you feel. Remove the "ifs", "hopefullys" and "should" and replace them with positive, assumptive language. Like most areas of our lives, our language is habitual. Considering the number of words available to us, most of us use a tiny number to interact and describe our experiences, and those words have a positive or negative valence. If our language tends to be negative, we need to make a conscious effort to use more neutral or positive language to replace the negative and rewire our brain.

By far the best way to do this is to role-play interactions before they happen. I've been involved in corporate training for many years and, without exception, people in training programs hate role-playing, but it is still the most effective way to replace new behaviour or language with old. It's all very well to tell someone to stop complaining, but if all they've ever done is complain they don't have positive habits or language to replace that negativity.

Pay attention to what you say, to yourself and others, and catch and correct yourself when you use negative or unhelpful language. In the beginning, you may surprise yourself with how often you get in your own way and drag yourself and others down. Try putting an elastic band around your wrist. Every time you hear yourself complain or be overly negative snap the band on your wrist. This will help to break the negative patterns and may also make you laugh, especially if you find yourself snapping your wrist every minute or so! It won't hurt too much, but will help bring your negativity into your conscious awareness so you can change it and replace the negative comments and self-talk with neutral or more constructive language.

Another idea is to enlist the help of others to help you break your negative language patterns. The biggest challenge with negative language patterns, or any language patterns for that matter, is that we are not aware of them. Have you got a friend who uses the same phrases all the time but doesn't realise it? We all have favourite words or phrases that we use more than average. For example, I use the word "rigour" a lot, although I didn't realise it until it was pointed out to me! I've deliberately changed it in this book because it's not a common word and can sometimes cause confusion. The point is, we all have language signatures, but because they are habits we don't hear them, whereas other people around us often do. Ask your family and friends whether you have any stock phrases or words that you use a lot. If those words or phrases have a negative valance or undertone, such as, "Oh, I'm not sure" or "Not really my thing" or "Well, that's not going to happen," ask them to shout "Hobgoblin" at the top of their voice every time they hear you say it! You can choose any word you want, ideally one that makes you laugh, as this will further help to break down the negative language patterns. Obviously, if you say something in the middle of your best friend's wedding ceremony, ask your friends and family to exercise some restraint!

Over time your habitual language patterns will change so that you support yourself rather than sabotage yourself!

Get Practical

The only way to become unstuck is to change something about the situation that you are stuck in. As mentioned earlier, you may decide that you don't need to change everything or leave the situation completely – small tweaks and some reframing of mind-set can make a huge difference. But regardless of whether you are making small changes or big ones, change requires action.

Consider what practical tasks and issues you need to take care of to help you get from where you are to where you want to be quicker. Are there practical things you can do now that can help prepare you for the change and smooth your progress through the change? Are there any financial considerations that you need to think about? Consider reading Chapter 13 next on choices and try the mind map exercise.

Often making a list of all the things that need to get done can help. Not only does this offer a practical outline of all the issues you need to deal with, it breaks your goal or outcome down into bite-sized manageable chunks. This can help to remove some of the overwhelming feelings around the change and take some things off the list that shouldn't be there. As you tick things off the list you get to feel good, gather momentum and improve your self-confidence and self-belief as you take each forward step.

Finally, consider what you enjoy doing and do more of it. This may sound trite, but when we are making changes in one area of our life, it can easily destabilise the rest. Finding little ways to manage the transition as painlessly as possible is always wise. Stay connected to good friends and family, look after yourself physically, and find your happiness where you can. Consider who else could advise or support you through this change?

Appreciate Timing

Often, personal development or coaching books will advocate that you "give yourself a week or a month to prepare and then make the change". On one hand this suggestion makes sense, because it provides structure and puts a timeline to the change. Unfortunately, life rarely works out like that, plus it can add another level of stress to the process.

I recall when one of my coaching clients explained that her previous executive coach made her write out and sign up to a service agreement for her personal life! Isn't life stressful enough without having your own personal SLA? She had to itemise and schedule things like, "I will take two hours on a Monday to do my personal admin" and "one hour every day I will spend time with my husband."

The timing of your change is going to be personal and unique to you. If you are the sort of person who likes to plan things out, make lists and give yourself deadlines, then planning out the change may be helpful for you. But you also have to recognise that there is an element of timing that can 't be managed or planned for - and that second timing can easily derail the first.

Although change can take time, the moment of realisation that change *has* to occur usually happens in a split second. And no amount of planning can account for that. Your "enough is enough" moment may seem like a tiny, trivial situation to others, but cuts you to your core. I remember talking to one client and asking her what helped her finally get out of her toxic relationship. She said, "I heard someone say to me *'what's the point?'*" And that was enough. It was a totally innocuous question, but it was enough to flick the switch inside her to make the change.

That moment where we "wake up" and know that we need to extricate ourselves from a situation we are stuck in can come from anywhere: a stray comment from a friend, a billboard on the back of a bus, or, like me, an event that just pushes us over the edge.

When the student is ready, the teacher will appear.

–Buddhist proverb

In addition, when we are stuck we can remain stuck for years. It's therefore pretty unrealistic to imagine that we are going to become unstuck in a matter of days. The process of change is never linear and we will often take two steps forward and three steps back.

Progress has not followed a straight ascending line,
but a spiral with rhythms of progress and retrogression,
of evolution and dissolution.

–Johann Wolfgang von Goethe

In their book *Changing for Good* the authors, all prominent behavioural scientists, explored this spiral change process. Having reviewed every major change methodology, they concluded that change was not linear. When changing behaviour the individual will spiral through phases of progress and failure. This means there will be set-backs, moments of insecurity, feelings of concern over whether we've done the right thing. We need to embrace these stages as normal and expected parts of the change process. Give yourself the time you need to make the transition the way you want to and feel comfortable with.

Coping Strategies During the Transition

Getting out of a relationship or leaving a job takes time and it's not always easy or pleasant. It's important that you mentally prepare for the rough and tumble that almost certainly lies ahead. It may be difficult, stressful and painful, but take comfort that the other side is going to be better, for everyone involved.

Through my work I have often had to fire people. I've often been asked how I could do it because the automatic assumption is that it must be terrible – terrible to terminate someone's employment and terrible for the person losing their job. Sometimes it is, but sometimes it's a blessing and the person involved is genuinely relieved or happy. This is a great example of how our assumptions can expect something to be awful when actually the reverse can be true. When someone isn't right for an organisation, for whatever reason, and they struggle themselves to do anything about it, an "intervention" like this can be what is needed for the person (although they might not realise it at the time). I always say we shouldn't be so "fixed" on what we think is the best thing for another person, because we don't. When someone is liberated from a job that doesn't suit them, that they don't love or thrive in, regardless of whether that liberation was welcome at the time or not, it does provide that person with the opportunity to find something that does suit them – that they do love and thrive in. What was initially viewed as "disaster" can often be later described as, "The best thing that ever happened to me." Being fired was a gift not a curse. If are you are facing redundancy, have faith. Most people I fired went on to get much better jobs or start their own businesses and felt happier for it!

Where possible, develop your own coping strategies before you press the "Go" button on your change. Here are some strategies that may help:

- **Acknowledge what you are feeling and thinking in the moment** and know that it may be attached to the situation. In other words, it's not necessarily you but something you are reacting to because of your situation. I know when I have been going through major change I could be a bit barky and angry. Although I behaved badly occasionally, I knew it wasn't "me" and was able to march forward. Knowing that things may get tough from time to time plays a massive part in how we show up every day. Where possible, sit with the emotions and feelings, acknowledge them for what they are, and seek to separate them from you personally. So, what you might do is to sit quietly and acknowledge that you are feeling frustrated, angry, bitter, or whatever the emotion is. Say to yourself, "I am feeling X, Y, Z and that is okay because I understand it is the situation that is having an impact on me. The emotion I am feeling is not *me*, but how my body and mind are reacting. I feel it, acknowledge it and now I let it go."

- **Get resourceful!** – Remember the challenging times you have already lived through. What got you through? What resources – such as courage, confidence, patience or resilience – were useful to you? It might help to write a list here to remind you. Pull those through now; they will serve you well again. A good exercise you can do as frequently as you need is to sit quietly and use the relaxed breathing technique from Chapter 7 to calm your mind and body. Once you are calm, imagine a resource that you have used before e.g. courage. Remember the time where you used courage. What happened? Relive the situation in as much detail as you can recall, all the time breathing in and reconnecting to the courage you felt back then. Feel how it felt and how it empowered you and breathe that feeling in again, allowing it to fill your whole body and strengthen you. This can sound like an odd thing to do, but engage your imagination and just try it – you'll be surprised how your mind and body instinctively know how to create these resources. Whenever you need courage or any other positive resource, close your eyes and breathe that resource back into your body. If you need a resource that you don't remember ever experiencing, just imagine what it would feel like, or imagine someone else who has a really strong courage and what you notice about them – it still works.

- **Remember, nothing is permanent.** Take a helicopter view of your whole life, not just the change you are experiencing, and remember it will look different maybe next week, next month, next year. Now that you are taking control and making change for the better, the current turmoil is not permanent. Remind yourself of that when things are particularly challenging.

- **You are in control about whether you react or don't react.** Sometimes not reacting is the right thing to do and is just as powerful or smarter than reacting (even if you want to show you were right or want the last word!). Remember, there might not be much point anyway. If you are leaving your job, why get into an argument with your boss? If you are leaving your partner, why get into another fight? This removes a lot of the stress too. Seek to make your life as easy as possible during the transition.

You have to be willing to give up the life you have planned in order to receive the life that is waiting for you.

–Joseph Campbell

Additional Resources

Watch: My Facebook video clip on *"Are You Stuck"* to refresh you on the ideas in the chapter along with some additional tips.

Watch: *Educating Rita* starring Michael Caine and Julie Walters – an inspiring story of being stuck and finding a way out.

Read: *Full Catastrophe Living* by Jon Kabat Zinn is a manual for developing your own personal meditation practice and learning how to use mindfulness to promote improved health and healing in your own life.

Read: *Power of Habit by Charles Duhigg* – to help you better understand how habits are formed and how they can be broken.

Chapter 2
Pack Away Your Old Emotional Baggage

The feelings you have about your past and the things that have happened to you, which often have a negative effect on your behaviour and attitudes. Men aren't supposed to carry as much emotional baggage as women. [Yes, it really does say that last bit!]

(*The wildly inaccurate definition of "emotional baggage" according to the *Collins English Dictionary*)

Are you an over-sharer? When meeting someone for the first time, do you often find yourself sharing too much personal information, usually a negative experience? Do you seem to have favourite topics of conversation that always seem to come around, no matter what you are talking about? Do you often seem to bring conversation back to your story about how life isn't fair? Do you get bored of listening to yourself play the same tune, or do others get bored of listening to you? If anyone has ever rolled their eyes at you and said, "Oh no, not this story again. Give it a rest!" it's probably time to pack away your emotional baggage.

We all have emotional baggage. If you are an adult beyond your early 20s it's inevitable. It comes in various shapes and forms, but contrary to the Collins definition above, emotional baggage is a human phenomenon, not a female one! From my coaching and life experience I promise you men can carry just as much as women. It might not be on display on the roof rack, but it's certainly there, probably locked away in the boot!

We have all been through highs and lows that shape us into the people we are today – good and bad. If you look back at your life, like the chapters in a book, they can provide a varied and interesting read: different experiences, different relationships, different jobs, different cities, different friends, different hopes and dreams as we grow and develop. These experiences allow us to gain wisdom and help us to understand ourselves a little more. I often look back at old photographs from my past and I barely recognise myself or even remember the chapter! Most of us have had the experience of reminiscing with a friend and saying, "I was a different person then." It can really feel like a different life.

Of course, our life experiences result in our own unique story and help create wonderful and not so wonderful memories. Often we remember these stories and relay them to others from time to time. Our stories are a way of connecting to each other: "I used to be a bus driver." "Oh, did you? I used to be a bus driver too." They help us find common ground and build successful relationships, often with people who have similar stories. We feel comfortable with that person because we have things in common. Often we assume they understand us that little bit more because they have lived a similar life.

Most of the time the emotions we experience as we travel through each chapter can be neatly packed away once we transition to a new situation or stage. We pack away our wild single shenanigans (the good and bad) once we transition into a committed relationship, or we pack away the highs and lows of a marriage or relationship when we finalise the separation. But what happens when those emotions just won't stay in the suitcase? Or what happens when you're trailing your emotional baggage along behind you and you don't even realise it?

The term "emotional baggage" is probably most often used in connection to personal relationships – probably because this is an area of our life that is highly charged, intense and often deeply emotional for most of us. The thrill of meeting someone new, the disappointments, the hope, the fights, the making up – primarily it's an emotional journey. As a result, emotional baggage is often associated with previous or new relationships or experiences, although I've also met people with emotional work baggage too. Work baggage can include previous bad managers, redundancy, or being frequently overlooked for a promotion. It can apply to anything where we have experienced something emotionally challenging that we either haven't properly dealt with or don't want to deal with.

The First Step Toward Change

Like most things in life, we can't change it unless we recognise it and, where appropriate, own it as something we need to address. The first step, therefore, is to learn how to recognise badly packed emotional baggage in yourself and others so you can do something about it yourself and manage it, or avoid it, in others. I gave a few pointers at the start of the chapter but here are a few more signs.

Other signs to look out for in others:

- A negative repetition of how "bad things always happens to them", or how they "never have any luck". These types of negative universal generalisations indicate that the individual has formed some unhelpful assumptions about the future based on his or her past experiences.
- An unusually intense emotional reaction to a situation – especially when things don't go according to plan. An inappropriate emotional response to an event that doesn't seem to warrant such an extreme reaction may signal that you've inadvertently rummaged through their emotional baggage which has triggered an unexpected reaction. You may even hear people say, "Oh, I'm sorry, I don't know what came over me." It may also show up in a "paranoia" or an intense emotional reaction.
- Insecurity – the need for a person to constantly be told something is okay, or that they are good at what they do,

they look good etc. They are seeking external validation because they feel insecure. This is also sometimes exhibited with low self-esteem.

- Over-reliance on a partner or over-control of a partner. This can manifest as being "needy", where their sense of self comes from the other person rather than themselves.

Other signs to look out for that you may need to re-pack your own emotional baggage:

- Your "story" around various events in your life and what you've made these experiences mean, focusing on the negative. Do you still feel "wronged", "slighted", "mistreated", "cheated on" etc?
- You have a tendency to "sabotage" yourself if you notice absolutely anything that is similar to, or mirrors, something you have previously experienced. For example, let's say you're ready for a first date and…
  - He's late picking you up.
  - The song playing in the car when you get in reminds you of another horrendous first date.
  - When you get to the restaurant, he doesn't use his knife when he eats, eats loudly, or doesn't like his food touching which reminds you of someone else.
  - He calls you by an endearing nickname that a previous partner used for you.

  These or similar scenarios could trigger an internal, "Oh no, not again" response that means you write the person off before ever giving them a chance – just because they triggered emotional baggage about your own past.
- Your reaction or behaviour frustrates and confuses you.

You even hear yourself saying, "But, I can't help it" or "I can't help how I feel." If you "can't help it", chances are your emotional baggage is spilling out of its suitcase.

- You tend to blame a previous experience (or person) for making you "feel bad" or "feel the way you do", rather than taking responsibility for your role in the situation and the way you're reacting now.

Beware feelings of bitterness, resentment, guilt, anger, jealousy and revenge that you may develop. These can be extremely destructive emotions and behaviours that impact you far more than they impact anyone else – even if you may want them to. They get in the way of you packing your emotional bags and they eat away at who you really are. It's hard to move on and open yourself up to the rest of your journey, and the adventure it may bring, when you are holding on to a negative experience from your past. Hanging on to past upsets and pain, reliving them over and over again, is like drinking poison every day. The only person it harms is you. Stop drinking the poison, leave your bags at the door and live again.

There's a luggage limit to every passenger on a flight.
The same rules apply to your life.
You must eliminate some baggage before you can fly.

–Rosalind Johnson

Tips and Strategies

By now, you may be telling yourself, "Well, that's all very well for you to say, but it's not as easy as that. It's not easy to just let go of emotional baggage." I hate to burst your bubble, but actually it is. You just choose a different story; make what happened to you mean something positive; find your own silver lining, however slim or faint, and move on. We are not shaped by our experiences, we are shaped by what we choose to make those experiences mean about who we are, what we deserve, and what we are capable of. Take conscious control of that process instead of letting knee-jerk emotional reactions determine your present and your future.

Obviously, I'm not talking about severe emotional trauma that might come from abuse or some other really awful life experience. I'm talking about emotional baggage: the nonsense we make up to justify or explain what happened to us, that we then drag around and allow to infect everything it touches. If you are suffering from serious trauma, then I encourage you to seek help so you can lay those ghosts to rest, pack them away and move forward. Freedom could be around the corner and there are people who can support you and help you get there faster.

How you can help yourself:

- **Recognise and admit where your baggage is.** Quite often, this baggage is blamed on someone else or a previous situation. Take responsibility for your part. You don't need to "fall on your sword" over it, but acknowledge how you contributed to the situation or event. Appreciate the fact that you could probably have done better, behaved better or made better decisions. This acknowledgement and quiet internal acceptance of accountability helps you to move from victim to co-conspirator and allows you to better control how you feel about it.
- **Focus on the positive.** You are a product of all your previous experiences, good and bad. They have made you who you are today. Even the tough times delivered some benefit. It could be anything from, "It's made me more patient" to "It's made me more empathetic" to "I was able to help others." Even the darkest of experiences will have something positive to offer if you choose to find it. Identifying the benefits

can be instrumental in helping you to change "your story" around these events so that you can re-pack your baggage and move on.

- **Embrace the grief.** When your dreams are dashed or an experience doesn't work out as planned, you will always go through some kind of grieving process. This is normal and there is no right or wrong way to grieve, but it's absolutely essential for healing so embrace it. Go through the grieving process with an assurance that it's not permanent – it's just a transition from difficulty and loss to light and new beginnings. You don't have to stay a hostage of misery forever. You don't have to stay miserable and unhappy! It really is your choice.

- **Get help, look for support.** Talking is healthy and there are some wonderful therapists that can help you to re-pack your emotional baggage once and for all.

- **Be clear about your boundaries – what you will and will not tolerate**. If you don't have boundaries, then it's time to set some. Everyone makes mistakes and hindsight is great for berating yourself about what you could have or should have done, but it won't change the past. Learning from that past will, however, change your future, so dissect your mistakes with the impartial enquiry of a scientist so you can then create clear boundaries for yourself that will prevent a repeat performance. Know what you are willing to negotiate on and what are your "deal breakers", and you will be less likely to find yourself in a similar situation somewhere down the track.

- **Make sure you do work on your self-esteem/confidence** (see Chapter 10). If you need it, remember you are deserving and worthy of finding someone who loves you "just the way you are" and supporting you to be the best you can be.

- **Learning is critical.** Remember, if you don't learn from your mistakes then life has a funny way of sending you the same lesson in a more intense and often unpleasant package!

Beware closing yourself off to life. Setting boundaries is an important part of learning lessons, so that we don't repeat past errors. But make sure they reflect what you want and what you think will help you stay mentally and physically healthy. When you get hurt by life's lessons it can be easier to develop a "hardness". This protective layer tells the world, "Not me. Never again." Although understandable, this approach is likely to limit all the experiences of your life – not just the tough ones. By shutting yourself off from life you can easily become bitter and move further and further away from what you actually want and how you want to live your life. You need to be brave and open your heart, albeit with the right safeguards (boundaries) in place, so that you can fully experience the wonders that are waiting for you.

And, if you are wondering how you will know when you have neatly packed a little more of your emotional baggage – that's easy. You (or your relieved friends or colleagues) will realise you aren't talking about the situation much anymore. You will be able to reflect on it factually, as simply a chapter of your life, rather than an emotionally drenched synopsis of the whole book! And, finally, you will be able to give guidance and wise words of encouragement to others who might find themselves in similar situations, without being bitter, resentful, or stirring up uncomfortable thoughts and feelings. Congratulations! Lesson learned, bags packed. You are ready for new adventures and thrilling new beginnings.

And the best bit: once you've packed your baggage away neatly you can choose to put it in long term storage or dump it all together. If you're really lucky it might dump itself without you even realising!

Often our emotional baggage keeps us stuck and the glue that keeps us stuck is often a strong emotion. If you are still struggling with anger, grief or depression, chapters 3, 4 or 5 may help.

The past has no power to stop you from being present now.
Only your grievance about the past can do that.
What is grievance? The baggage of old thought and emotion.

–Lao Tzu

Additional Resources

Watch: My Facebook video clip on emotional baggage as a handy visual reminder for what's included in the chapter. Use this as a good refresher.

Watch: *Brene Brown's TED talk on the Power of Vulnerability.* For too long we've been hoodwinked into believing vulnerability is a sign of weakness and, sadly, this is especially true for boys and men. This presentation illuminates just how wrong that idea is and how vulnerability requires courage, but the rewards are worth it.

Read: *The Biology of Belief: Unleashing the Power of Consciousness, Matter & Miracles* by Bruce H. Lipton.

Read: *Breaking the Habit of Being Yourself* by Dr Joe Dispenza

Chapter 3
Shifting Anger

Anger is a killing thing: it kills the man who angers,
for each rage leaves him less than he had been before
- it takes something from him.

–Louis L'Amour

Do you spend a lot of your time angry? Is your anger directed toward a single event or person, or do you just find that a lot of situations make you angry? Is anger holding back your career? Is it causing upset and disconnection in your personal relationships? If so, it may be time to understand your triggers better, so you can reduce your anger response to those things that really warrant it.

Anger is a normal emotional response. It is an emotional signpost that tells us that something is wrong and needs our attention. But it's not somewhere we should live! Everyone gets angry from time to time: someone cuts us off on the motorway, or we come back to our car to find a parking ticket under the windscreen wiper. Anger is usually triggered when our values have been violated. In other words, someone or something has not behaved or worked out as expected. When our expectations of a person or situation are not met, we get frustrated, fearful, upset, anxious, hurt or defensive. All of which can eventually manifest as anger, especially if the person or situation persists. Escalating change and increased expectations do, however, mean that more and more of us are spending too much time in anger. Our fuses seem shorter. Everyone is in a rush to get somewhere and our patience and tolerance seems to be dropping. Whether we are in the car and someone is getting in our way, or we're in the wrong queue in the supermarket, our rise to anger can be all too quick and frankly over the top.

Sitting in, or living in, the anger is exceptionally bad for your physical and mental health. Anger floods your body with cortisol – the stress hormone – and elevated cortisol levels have been linked to a variety of serious health problems such as obesity, diabetes, high blood pressure, heart disease, cancer, depression and dementia. There is a proven scientific relationship between cortisol and negative emotions such as anger. Plus, increased levels of cortisol are likely to induce more "negative" emotions which creates a vicious cycle. Anger is therefore very bad for our health. It can also be exhausting and rob us of energy and our enjoyment of life.

This can be highlighted by a lovely little fable…

One day Buddha was walking through a village. A very angry and rude young man came up and began insulting him. "You have no right teaching others," he shouted. "You are as stupid as everyone else. You are nothing but a fake." Buddha was not upset by these insults. Instead, he asked the young man, "Tell me, if you buy a gift for someone and that person does not accept it, to whom does the gift belong?" The man was surprised to be asked such a strange question and answered, "It would belong to me, because I bought the gift." The Buddha smiled and said, "That is correct. And it is exactly the same with your anger. If you become angry with me and I do not get insulted, then the anger remains yours."

First Steps Toward Change

The real purpose of anger is to alert you to a possible challenge that you may need to handle. It may be that you need to have a hard conversation with someone and explain how their actions have affected or upset you. It may be that you need to seek an apology or a better understanding of what actually happened, or it may be that you need to "get over yourself" and just let it go. None of us are perfect and, perhaps more importantly, we can never know what personal or professional dramas the other person is dealing with on the day. Remember, we only know our story. We don't know their full story or context (even if we think we do). We may never know why someone behaved badly or why a situation turned to custard in a heartbeat, but we can still control our reaction to it.

The first steps are to remember:

- **It's very difficult, if not impossible, to regain your equilibrium once you are already angry** – the energy (e) is already in motion in your body, hence the term "emotion". Remove yourself from the situation or take yourself away from the other person before you say or do something you regret. Allow yourself some space to regain control in your own time.

- **Once out the way, consider what part you played, or could have played, in the situation**. Anger is often the result of feeling as though something has been "done to us". We are therefore the victim of the situation, which in turn often amplifies the anger because we feel powerless. Powerlessness is not helpful. Instead, consider how you contributed to the situation and own it. You don't need to shout if from the rafters or admit it to the other person – just be honest with yourself. Consider what you could have done differently to avoid the situation. Owning your part, however small, helps to immediately defuse some of the intensity of the anger and, more importantly, helps to put you back in control so you are no longer a "victim".

- **Accept the fact that people don't always act reasonably or nicely.** There isn't always a reason, there isn't always an excuse, and you may never get to the bottom of why it happened or why someone behaved in a certain way. Sometimes, shit happens! Don't take it personally amplify the reasons that you make it mean, or start the storytelling – just move on.

- **Once you have put yourself back in control i.e. decided how you are going to manage your reaction rather than**

being at the mercy of your reaction, AND you have acknowledged that you may never know why someone has acted the way they have, you can now decide:

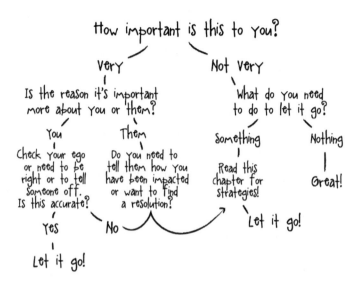

How important is this to you?

Very / Not very

Very →
Is the reason it's important more about you or them?

You / Them

You →
Check your ego or need to be right or to tell someone off. Is this accurate?

Yes / No

Yes →
Let it go!

Them →
Do you need to tell them how you have been impacted or want to find a resolution?

Not very →
What do you need to do to let it go?

Something / Nothing

Something →
Read this chapter for strategies!

Nothing →
Great!

Let it go!

- How important is this to you? How important is the person to you?
- If they are important you may need to invest in some self-reflection and spend some time and effort sorting it out. Why wouldn't you?
- If you are working something out with someone, make sure you give them the space to make amends Calling a truce, or a suspension of accusation, is helpful to allow things to course-correct. If you are constantly calling someone out because anger is still driving you, you are unlikely to get the other person to make the effort. What's the point if you are still going to be angry with them?
- If the situation or the person is not that important to

you, then why would you bother getting angry about it? Often in these situations it's not the event or person that's causing the anger, but your own ego hanging on to "your right" to be angry! For example, you may be embarrassed or feel silly, but rather than brush it off you overcompensate and fly into a rage instead. Of course, this can so easily make matters worse as you look even more silly for the overreaction! Vocabulary or thinking such as, "Who do they think they are?" Or "They can't do that to someone like me!" are sure signs your ego has stepped forward and is about to make matters worse! These types of phrases indicate that you are more worried about what something "looks like" than what you actually feel!

- Consider writing down what happened to help you gain clarity. You may want to write a letter to the other person explaining your point of view. However, this can't be an angry rant full of blame and recrimination – it needs to be a sane explanation of the issue from your point of view. If you can't write that yet, then you need to work on defusing more of the toxicity of your anger before putting pen to paper. Often this can reduce anger levels and you don't even need to send it! In fact, I would encourage you not to send the letter at all. If you are convinced you want to, or need to, send the letter, then write it, put it aside for two weeks and then review it again. The space will almost always make you glad you didn't send it!

- **Use the drama rating scale from Chapter 7, and remember not to embellish your story** to warrant a more intense emotional response. Too often we work ourselves up to more and more intense feelings of anger, simply by going over the situation again and again in our minds (or we take counsel from others who help us "stay in this anger space" as they heap on more storytelling or emotions. This is not helpful and will only serve to sustain and amplify the anger. Come back to the present and busy yourself in the here and now.

Tips and Strategies

Every time you get angry, you poison your own system.

–Alfred A. Montapert

Anger is an incredibly useful emotion in the right environment and there are certainly situations that demand it. The key is to use it intermittently when you decide to use it, rather than living in anger and being at the mercy of this highly toxic emotion. The following tips and strategies can help you take charge and stay in the moment.

Practise Forgiveness and Compassion

Most of us consider that forgiveness and compassion is something we give to others. It can feel as though we are letting the other person "off the hook". Needless to say, this can be challenging, especially when someone has done something really terrible or caused serious problems or unhappiness. I know that forgiving is hard and some of us will "never forgive the unforgiveable". If that's you, then maybe that's fine, but ONLY if it doesn't continue to cause you any kind of emotional distress. If you find yourself sitting with anger for hours, days, months, even years, then I would strongly encourage you to give forgiveness and compassion a try. We might say, "But, I can't help it. I just can't stop being angry" or, "It always makes me angry when I think about it…"

But forgiveness rarely has anything to do with the other person. It's something we can learn to give to ourselves. If you are angry at someone or angry about an event or situation – whether that situation happened this morning or 20 years ago – it's you who is suffering from that anger. The "event" doesn't care! And the other person probably doesn't care either. It's you who's distraught, churning the event or conversation over and over again in your head, replaying the situation constantly to relive the upset. Every time you do, your physiology alters internally as you release cortisol into your system. High levels of cortisol in your body cause illness and disease – and it's you who will suffer from those illnesses and disease, not the other person! That's crazy! Hanging on to anger, resentment, revenge, bitterness or upset is like doing shots of poison every morning and wondering why you are sick, tired and unhappy!

Director of the Stanford Forgiveness Project, Dr Fred Luskin, demonstrated the power of forgiveness and empathy when he brought a small group of Protestants and Catholics together who had all lost loved ones in Northern Ireland during the "troubles". Even though their losses had occurred over 20 years earlier, the grief and anger was still palpable. It had not diminished with time. The first breakthrough of the week-long project occurred when both sides realised that they shared the same grief and sadness. At the end of the week, participants reported that they felt lower levels of hurt, anger and depression and they experienced a 35 per cent reduction in physiological symptoms of emotional stress, such as irregular sleep, loss of appetite, low energy and physical aches and pains.

Learn to forgive others and yourself. It's just better for your health and happiness.

Dilute Your Anger to Disappointment

Realistically, if you have lived with anger as a pretty constant companion, then letting go of it is going to be a process. It's not something we can just switch off – at least not in the early days of trying to make positive changes.

The tricky thing about anger is that once it's arrived, all bets are off! Trying to manage that in the moment is a little like shutting the barn door once the horse has bolted. It's too late – the physiological signals that herald anger in the body are already in motion. But you can tone it down and dilute it once it's arrived, so that you don't let it screw things up or you don't live in that toxic state.

A good strategy is to turn the volume down by turning the emotion of "anger" into "disappointment".

Disappointment is a much softer, calmer emotion that allows you to be more reflective, so you can better deal with the fallout. Quite often, we make assumptions or have beliefs about others that just don't stack up when really questioned or challenged. In truth, the other person's behaviours are often simply a manifestation of something that they are going through or feeling that may actually have nothing to do with us – we were just in the wrong place at the wrong time! Remember, anger can be the mask for something else, so always try and look behind the veil to consider what might really be going on.

A close friend of mine, Julie, wanted to get married to her boyfriend, Chris – only Chris' sister, Linda, didn't like Julie very much. Linda was good friends with Chris' previous girlfriend and her loyalty lay with her friend, not her brother's new partner. And you know what – that's absolutely fair enough – to a point. These kinds of shack-ups are very common when people break up and those around them have to work out who they are going to stay in contact with.

What isn't fair enough, however, is that on their wedding day Linda told Julie that she would never be accepted and the rest of the family didn't like her either. It was a brutal thing to say on such a special day and really tough for Julie to hear. Julie was shocked, deeply hurt and upset, and then really, *really* angry! Linda seemed to have no problem enjoying the hospitality of the day, paid for by both Chris and Julie. Needless to say, Julie was livid for weeks. *Who does that on someone's wedding day?* For Julie, her anger was understandable, but it was polluting her sense of joy and happiness at being married – especially as it was Chris's own sister who had caused so much distress. Instead of focusing on the unreasonableness of the situation and trying to figure out how someone so close to Chris could be so unkind to both of them on such an important day, Julie consciously shifted her anger to disappointment. She chose to be disappointed in Linda rather than angry at her. Standing in Linda's shoes she was able to appreciate her sadness at the loss of the relationship between her friend and her brother. All the shared events that she thought she was going to enjoy: perhaps shared holidays, shared raising of children, shared play dates etc. This allowed Julie to end up feeling sorry for her and appreciating her sense of loss. It didn't alter what was said or when it was said, but it allowed Julie to let the anger go and get on with her new life with Chris. And the saddest part of all is that Linda's harsh words and insensitivity didn't change anything between Julie and Chris, but it did change the relationship Linda ended up having with her brother and his new wife.

If we are capable of dissolving anger that quickly simply by altering the story, or choosing to see the story from a different angle or other person's perspective, then why wouldn't we use that strategy to change the strength of the emotion so we don't wallow in our own anger?

Come up with a story that will allow you to tone down your anger to disappointment, so you can reflect on the situation and get into positive action.

Beware! Revenge can often walk hand in hand with anger. It's another destructive emotion that can eat away at you and become all-consuming, not only in an emotional sense, but also physically. It can be draining, mainly for you, not the other person. If revenge rears its ugly head, remember it's a tool that will ultimately damage you more than it will damage the other person. You might believe in karma instead: what goes around comes around!

While seeking revenge, dig two graves - one for yourself.

–Douglas Horton

Choose to Release the Other Person From Your Expectations

Anger is often the result of someone not behaving as you expected or wanted them to behave. But we can never know what is truly going on for another person, or why they acted or didn't act in a certain way. We have no real control over what others think, so rather than getting upset and making ourselves ill over the situation, we can chose to release the other person from our expectations. I have had a personal experience with this kind of situation, where someone I had worked with and with whom I'd enjoyed a really good professional relationship for years, behaved really badly towards me. I went to the place of feeling let down, disappointed beyond belief, betrayed, you name it. It felt awful and impacted me for months. It gnawed away at the back of my mind. I tried to rationalise it, tried to let it go, but it just kept coming back and I would re-experience the hurt and disappointment all over again. The following technique helped me remove it completely.

For this technique to really deliver benefit and help you to diminish or dispel your feelings of anger, you need to articulate exactly what it was that you expected and then release the other person from that expectation. This will help you to better appreciate why you are angry in the first place and help disconnect you from your upset. Often, when we bring our unconscious expectations or assumptions into conscious awareness, we can see them for what they really are. They are often silly, unrealistic, or perhaps simply expecting too much of the other person at that time. Even if they feel and remain valid, you can use this technique to sever your emotional connection to the person or event to diminish the anger you feel. Remember, we don't always know the full story that played out for them at the time.

This technique is best used as you are imagining the person standing in front of you, or perhaps imagine them sitting in a chair while you are standing in front of them. Find somewhere that you won't be disturbed, so you can say what you need to say out loud. Saying it out loud will help dispel the emotion more than running through an internal dialogue. Here is an example of what you might say to that person (fit your own words around the story):

"My expectation of you is that you would look out for me and be loyal."

"But, you did not do that."

"You let me down and I can't believe you would do that to me."

"You are not who I thought you were."

Once you have articulated why you feel so upset, say, "I cancel or remove my expectation of you." Swipe your arm across your body in a downwards motion as you say the words. Imagine you are rubbing the expectation off a blackboard.

Once you remove or wipe away your expectation the upset won't feel so intense. You may need to repeat this process a couple of times. It is possible that doing this exercise will help you to better appreciate why you are so upset and you will gain new insights into the situation. If so, try changing the dialogue so that you get to the real heart of what it is that's causing you the distress and then cancel that expectation too.

Visualisation

If you are still struggling to relinquish your rage, or it keeps rising up in you, or is frequently triggered, use the following technique to calm yourself and release some anxiety.

- Close your eyes and use the breathing technique explained in Chapter 7 to help get yourself centred and calm.
- Visualise the person or event you are angry with and relive the situation in your mind's eye. Engage with your surroundings, when it happened, the situation, the words that were used – everything that you observed and heard

at the time.

- Visualise a box at your feet or nearby, move toward the box and open it.

- Next, re-connect to the visualisation of your negative experience – faces, voices, words, the environment, and anything else that is connected to it. Visually put everything into the box.

- Visualise yourself slowly closing the box, padlocking it and securing a strap around the box to keep it tightly closed. Attach a hook to the strapping at the top of the box.

- Now visualise a hot air balloon coming down from the sky, hovering just above your box. Hook the box to the bottom of the balloon. Watch the box rise up into the sky and slowly float away. Watch it for as long as you can as it disappears over the horizon, out of sight.

- Make sure you are using nice, slow breathing throughout. Once it's out of sight, continue with your relaxed breathing and visualise a nice experience that you have had recently (think of this before you start). Make sure you visualise it in all its glory including the colours, sounds, smells and pictures. Continue your relaxed breathing.

- You may have to do this visualisation technique a number of times depending on the situation, but give it a go, it really works!

Visualisation Technique

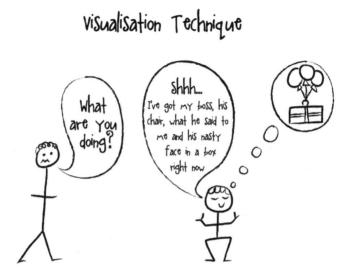

It's practically impossible to look at a penguin and feel angry.

–Joe Moore

Additional Resources

Watch: My Facebook video clip on anger is a good go-to visual reminder of what you can do in the moment to defuse the emotion.
Watch: *Anger, Compassion, and What it Means to be Strong* by Russell Kolts, who explores how many of us use anger as way of avoiding uncomfortable feelings.
Watch: *Blame* by Brene Brown as she considers why we blame others, how it sabotages our relationships, and why we desperately need to move beyond this toxic behaviour.
Read: *The Dance of Anger* by Dr Harriet Lerner who identifies the true sources of anger and how to use it as a powerful vehicle for creating lasting change.

Chapter 4
Wrestling With Guilt

Negative emotions like loneliness, envy, and guilt have an important role to play in a happy life; they're big, flashing signs that something needs to change.

–Gretchen Rubin

Is guilt a regular part of your existence? Do you find yourself agreeing to things you don't want to out of guilt? Do you berate yourself over something you did or didn't do? Do you put yourself in difficult situations in an attempt to make yourself feel better about something you feel you did wrong? Are you trying to redress some cosmic balance? Guilt is a normal human experience that tells us we may have taken a wrong turn, but if you find yourself wallowing in guilt, or constantly finding new and novel ways to berate yourself over the things you did or didn't do, think or feel, then this section may help you to let go.

Most of us experience guilt from time to time. Perhaps we behave badly to a friend, family member or our partner, or we do something or don't do something we should have. It's very easy to feel guilt over our health, when we know we are eating too much of the wrong foods and not doing enough exercise. We can feel guilt around our careers: perhaps we are not progressing fast enough or we stepped on a few people to progress faster. And, of course, being a parent is a hotbed of guilt! This is true for both parents, but can be especially relentless for mothers. Stay at home mothers feel guilty for staying at home and working mothers feel guilty for working! Society, the media, friends, family and strangers can all trigger our sense that we might be failing in some way.

Personally, I lived with a lot of guilt until I was exactly 40 years old. Although I can't put my finger on exactly why it finally disappeared, it was almost certainly down to the type of self-reflection and learning I've shared in this book – especially the insights around "hindsight" (if only we knew then what we know now). Unfortunately for me, I waited a little too long to let go of my guilt. Please don't make the same mistake. Ditch the guilt, it will free you.

As I mentioned in the preface, by the time I was born my Mum was ill with a degenerative brain disorder, although neither she nor my dad knew about it. My entire childhood "reality" was Mum being distant, aloof and behaving strangely. I knew she loved me, because she was my mother, so she had to, but she never told me herself, although other people assured me she did. Perhaps unsurprisingly, we had no particular relationship. The contact we did have was tempestuous – especially as I entered my teens. She tried to mask her illness by drinking, so between her condition, the alcohol, and my hormones, our communication consisted almost exclusively of shouting matches. We very rarely talked and, looking back, I think I was just scared but covered it up by either not being around or not being very nice when I was around.

I resented the fact that my siblings (who were at least 15 years older than me) had experienced her being normal and I hadn't. But, even during these years no one knew what was wrong with her, or even if there was anything medically wrong with her. All I knew was that my mum was different. She wasn't like my friends mums and I didn't like that. By the time I was 13 she was sectioned and sent to an institution. She died when I was 24 years old.

After visiting her in nursing homes for many years it was clear she was ill and finally everything started to make more sense. And that's when the guilt really set in. She had not been diagnosed early enough, probably because the doctors were just finding out about the condition. But that didn't make me feel better. I constantly felt guilty about our relationship and the way I'd behaved and this guilt continued long after she died. Suffice to say, I'm extremely experienced in the guilt department!

Part of my journey in coming to terms with my childhood and the 50/50 possibility that I may inherit her condition involved a lot of personal development and soul searching. I also actively sought out tools and techniques (many of which are in this book) to help me assimilate my experiences, accept them and move on.

Today, I often come across guilt working with coaching clients. It's not always visible in the first few sessions, as it tends to be something that courses underneath the highway of life, but it can certainly get in our way. The guilt we feel can be a nagging discomfort over something small that may show up from time to time, or it can be a permanent companion that colours our entire life.

Permanent, pervasive guilt can lead to low self-esteem and feelings of worthlessness. We come to believe that our actions or behaviours are somehow unforgivable and we need to be punished indefinitely for being such a "bad person". Depending on our religious upbringing we can add another layer to the guilt by convincing ourselves we are going to hell! I went to a convent, so was sure I'd be struck down by lightning and sent "downstairs" for my sins.

First Steps Toward Change

Before you emotionally flay yourself for something you did or didn't do in the past, there are a few things to know about guilt. Everyone can suffer from it at one point or another – none of us are perfect human beings. Everyone has done something or said something they wish they hadn't. Guilt is meant to be a signpost or warning system to help us avoid making the same mistakes again it's not a place to pitch a tent!

Guilt can also be the driving force behind other emotions such as frustration, anger, bitterness etc. Often, as we wrestle with our internal beliefs and value system around what we have done or said, it can be so challenging that we seek to externalise the feelings and find others to blame instead. This is not helpful. The only way to dissolve guilt is to accept our own failings, take responsibility for them and let them go. That may produce an apology from you or it may not. Deciding anger and blame are easier is a mistake that you will pay the price for, through elevated cortisol and stress levels and potentially resulting in behaviour that you might not like in yourself. It also takes up valuable room for all the good positive stuff!

Guilt can also pollute our decision making and, depending on the size of our misdemeanour, can lead to irrational choices we wouldn't normally make. It's almost like we gravitate to the worst possible decision, knowing it will lead to the worst possible outcome for us, which will somehow balance the books and assuage our guilt. I've come across divorcing couples where the "leaving" party agrees to a far more generous settlement than would be appropriate, just so they can feel less guilty about leaving. Children who feel guilty about an aging parent will decide to move that parent into their home in an effort to assuage the guilt. Guilt can drive people to do things that aren't right for them or the other person they are trying to feel less guilty about! And ironically, such irrational choices rarely help in alleviating the guilt, and even it does the effects are short lived.

Tips and Strategies

Guilt is anger directed at ourselves.

–Peter McWilliams

Guilt isn't a switch that you can flick on or off. It's more a gradual process of acceptance that you are not perfect, and that's OK. Below are some tips and ideas that can collectively help you to let go of your guilt and move on with your life constructively.

- **We always do the best we can with what we have.** Whatever you did or didn't do, you must accept that human beings will always do the best they can with the resources they have at the time. So, before you go beating yourself up, acknowledge that you were probably trying to do the right thing – even if that "right thing" didn't turn out so well. Perhaps you just didn't have the knowledge or skills or insights that would have allowed you to handle the situation differently.

  For years, I felt guilt about my mum, my behaviour, and the fact that we didn't really have a "normal" mother/daughter relationship. But I didn't know she was ill. She didn't even know she was ill for long enough. We both did the best we could with the resources we had at the time. In her case, her resources as an adult were diminishing as the disease altered her behaviour and personality. As for me, the rational part of my brain capable of making smart choices and accurately assessing the world around me wasn't even fully developed. So even if I had known, I'm not convinced I would have known how to deal with it. Even the medical professionals didn't know how to deal with it – most hadn't even heard of what she had – so there is no wonder I wasn't very good at managing it! Plus, like all teenagers, I was growing up and that was confusing enough! It was a perfect storm that neither of us had much control over.

If you've behaved badly in the past, cut yourself some slack and realise that whilst it didn't work out well you were probably doing the best you could at the time. Our life is full of various paths on our journey, it's not really very surprising that we take the wrong path now and again. The key is to realise it's the wrong path and get back on the right one as soon as you can. Choose to let go of the guilt. Try the visualisation technique to release rage in Chapter 2, only this time put your guilt in the basket of your hot air balloon and let it drift away.

- **Hindsight may be "a wonderful thing" but it's not very useful when it comes to guilt.** When we are on our guilt trip we can easily replay the whole situation over and over again in our heads – turning up the volume and emotion with each repeat. We cycle through what happened in the past so we re-experience the shame and regret. If only we could go back, knowing what we know now, we would have done it differently. Right?

Instead of using hindsight as a tool to further chastise yourself, celebrate it. If you know that you wouldn't behave that way now, then you are clearly a different person to the one who behaved badly. Guilt is only possible if the experience you feel guilty about actually changed you. If it hadn't, you wouldn't be feeling the guilt. Perhaps you are older, a little wiser, have more knowledge or information than you did then, or you've mellowed a little, become more resilient, or have expanded your life experience. Whatever is different, you are different, so to continue punishing the new you for a mistake made by the old you doesn't really seem fair does it? Let it go.

- **Check you aren't feeling "false guilt".** False guilt is guilt that actually doesn't belong to you. I see this in my coaching work more than you might think. We know if guilt is ours, right? Not always. Often a person can assume someone else's guilt and carry it as though it were their own. For example, a parent can often feel guilty when their child behaves badly – and this can still happen when their child is an adult themselves. It can also happen when the individual in question doesn't take accountability for what they did, so someone else in their vicinity will carry that guilt on their behalf. If you recognise this, give the guilt back, it's not yours to own. The other person needs to take responsibility, so that they can move forward and continue to develop as an adult human being. But regardless of whether they do or not, the guilt is not yours, so return it to its rightful owner immediately.

When someone we love behaves badly we can feel responsible – particularly if they refuse to accept liability and apologise. This can be especially true for our children, since we literally created that child. By accepting guilt on their behalf, you are effectively shielding them from the consequences of their own behaviour. But, no one really grows up until they appreciate the consequences of their actions. If you are carrying someone else's guilt, pass it back, metaphorically or physically!

- **We are not our behaviour.** Remember, guilt is usually about something you have done or said, or something you should have done but didn't. We feel guilt for our actions and behaviours, but our actions and behaviours are not necessarily who we are. We can do and say things in the moment because of other stuff going on in our lives – a death, illness, stress, or difficult relationships – they can all be drivers that move us away from who we really are inside and transform us into something or someone that we don't recognise. In other words, the way we behaved, even if it wasn't great, doesn't make us a horrible person, it just means we said something or did something what wasn't great at that particular time. Make sure you disconnect the behaviour from the "you" inside – they aren't always congruent.

This isn't about letting ourselves off the hook for bad behaviour, but it allows us to remember that, "I am a good person but I did something stupid" rather than "I did something stupid so I am a bad person." This is a very important distinction because it allows us to isolate the incident, rather than allowing it to negatively impact our self-esteem and sense of self. Ask yourself, "If I had my time again would I have handled it differently?" or "Would I handle it differently in the future?" If the answer is yes, then it shows that the problem lies not with you as a person, it was your behaviour or action at that time that you regret. Guilt is an emotion, not a personality trait. It's something that gets created by us and it can be un-created by us too.

Brene Brown would say that guilt is *focused on behaviour* i.e. "I did something bad," whereas shame is *focused on you* i.e. "I am bad." They are two different concepts that you shouldn't mix up, the latter being incredibly self destructive.

Separating the behaviour from the person is also a useful technique when other people have behaved badly towards you. This way you can isolate the behaviour without impacting how you feel about the person. Something may be going on for them that you have no idea about. Remember forgiveness and compassion in Chapter 3. (Obviously, if you are constantly doing this to minimise someone's bad behaviour then it may actually just be the person!)

- **Don't let "absence guilt" make up scenarios that may or may never have happened.** Let me give you an example: I coached one man who was in a relationship and decided to call it a day. A few months later he heard that his ex was going out with a guy who was treating her really badly and she was incredibly unhappy in her relationship. Absence guilt is the nonsense we create to make that our fault! The narrative goes something like this: "OMG, my ex is in a terrible relationship. If only I'd not broken up with him/her they would be OK. Oh, I'm such a terrible person." Of course, this is ridiculous. For a start, you are not anyone's saviour, nor can you take responsibility for someone else's choices and decisions. This approach also assumes that you (who didn't want to go out with this person any more) is a better option for your ex than their current partner. But maybe your ex needed to get a "wake-up call" and realise that he or she is worth more than both of you?! No one wants to be in a relationship with someone who's there only because they feel sorry for them!

Our brains are very good at spinning stories when guilt comes to town. We can beat ourselves us and look for evidence that anything is our fault if we look hard enough (remember "Confirmation Bias"). Stop being a martyr. Instead, ask yourself a few questions. In the situation above you might ask:

- Did your partner have a choice about who he/she went out with after you?
- Do you think they would have listened to your opinion on their choice had you given it?
- Do you think at some point they might have been able to make the decision to stop going out with that person before the situation became toxic?
- So, at what point are they accountable for their own choices, regardless of the circumstances? Sometimes we have to let people make their own choices and their own decisions while we make ours. We can't be responsible for everyone, we can only be good citizens as we try and make our way through life.
- Considering all of the above, was it really your fault?

- **Watch out for history being re-written!** Quite often, someone else's version of events may look and sound very different to our own. People remember different things based on their beliefs, values, and what they considered important about the event. No two witness statements of a crime are ever the same, because we each see and experience something slightly different. As a result, sometimes people re-write history at the expense of someone else to make themselves feel better.

I have a friend who climbed Kilimanjaro with two friends. Although they all got to the top and raised a lot of money for charity, the trip itself was a nightmare. Physical challenges such as these often bring out people's "true colours" and the two friends ended up hating each other, with my friend caught in the middle. In truth, no one behaved particularly well as they were put under increasing physical strain. Thankfully, everyone got home safely, although the friendships never recovered. Months later, my friend was listening as one of the girls was telling someone else what happened on the mountain. She was genuinely taken aback as she listened to her "version" of events, and heard how radically different it was to her own memory of what happened. If you don't remember something from the past it might be because it never actually happened! Research has proved that all of us are susceptible to "false memories", whereby we can be influenced or open to suggestions based on things that didn't even happen.

- **It's never too late to apologise and make amends.** If something is still upsetting you or worrying you, regardless of how long ago it was, and you feel you want to sort it out, take the bull by the horns and apologise. The other person can either accept your apology or not and, to be honest, both outcomes are fine. Your effort to say sorry and your willingness to accept responsibility for your part in the situation will help to disperse any residual guilt you feel. What the other person decides to do with your apology is down to them and is "their stuff" not yours.

Remember, it is the past that connects you to guilt, not guilt that connects you to your past. No amount of torturing yourself is going to change what happened. If the relationship your behaviour impacted is important to you, then do whatever you can to make amends so you can get yourself to a better, more balanced state of mind around the incident. Carrying it like a millstone around your neck isn't the answer. Flogging has long since been outlawed, so forgive yourself. You screwed up, welcome to the human race! Let it go.

Beware family guilt! Often those who love us the most are the best at knowing just what buttons to push and when to press them for maximum impact. This can be very upsetting and hurtful. Parents, children or even distant relatives can be masters at pushing the "guilt button" – and it is often the worst kind of guilt, because we are left wondering if there is a grain of truth in their barbs. If a family member says anything like, "You know I'd do anything for you, but…" or "You know I just want you to be happy, but…" then ready yourself for the "family guilt card". No one can make you feel guilty without your permission, so see it for what it is and edit accordingly. Try re-reading Chapter 2 on Emotional Baggage. Pay particular attention to "boundaries". Remember, this is your life. It's up to you to set your own boundaries so other people don't take liberties and try to manipulate you with guilt – even loved ones.

Guilt is to the spirit, what pain is to the body.

— **Elder David A. Bednar**

Additional Resources

Watch: My Facebook video on "Dealing with Guilt" as a quick recap of the topics in the chapter to help you deal with guilt in the moment.

Watch: *Shame, Guilt and the Power of Empathy* by Brene Brown

Read: *Daring Greatly* by Brene Brown

Read: *Remember That? No You Don't. Study Shows False Memories Afflict Us All* in Time magazine and watch the video at the bottom of the article about a woman who experienced amnesia and how happy she became in the present because she couldn't remember the past!

Chapter 5
Managing Anxiety, Stress, Depression Or Sadness

Boredom, anger, sadness, or fear are not 'yours,' not personal.
They are conditions of the human mind.
They come and go. Nothing that comes and goes is you.

–Eckhart Tolle

Do you wrestle with anxiety, stress, depression or sadness? Do you ever experience panic attacks or is there more a low level of constant anxiety that you experience? Have you just come to accept that you are stressed, as though it's the new normal of the modern world? Do you find yourself feeling blue more than you'd like? Does your sadness or depression feel heavy to you, as though you are wearing a thick cloak of melancholy that is weighing you down and holding you back? Would you like to know how to remove that cloak, even for a few hours so you can give yourself a break? Would you like you get rid of it for good?

Before we begin, it's worth pointing out that this chapter is directed specifically to those who feel anxiety, stress, depression or sadness *sometimes*. Perhaps you find yourself in the occasional funk and could do with some ideas about how to pull away from the negativity into a more positive mental place? If those feelings are a permanent fixture in your life, or even feel as though they are, then it's very likely you are going to need specialist support, so please make an appointment to see your doctor or a therapist.

Anxiety, sadness and even depression are all a normal part of being human. We experience difficulties and challenging situations that often warrant that emotional response. If we didn't know sadness, we wouldn't be able to appreciate happiness in quite the same way. We need the dichotomies of life to really experience life. Emotions are, however, energies in motion, so they are meant to pass. Often, when we feel anxious, sad or depressed, we can get stuck in that darkness. If that sounds familiar to you, then this chapter may help you gain a new perspective so you can navigate your way out of these, often debilitating, emotional states.

It's important to acknowledge that the world we live in is actually pretty stressful. Most of us have to make more decisions by lunchtime than our grandparents made all week! We are expected to juggle endless priorities without a murmur and just "soldier on". In that respect, is it really any wonder that we experience greater levels of anxiety, stress, sadness and depression? Our brains and bodies are often pushed to the max on a daily basis as we try to plough through the "stuff" we have to deal with on our endless to-do list.

It's clear that we need to learn and practice how to manage ourselves in order to remain healthy in body and mind. Some people are better at this than others, and those who struggle can find it incredibly difficult and life limiting. Whilst these emotional states are big, complex subjects, I have tried to pull out some of the simpler reasons around your mind and body physiology and what happens when we experience one of these negative states. The important thing to know is that all of us suffer with one or more of these states at some point in our lives. However, when we experience these emotions for longer periods it can be tough, very tough. All of these emotions can affect our sleep, appetite and physical and mental health.

The bizarre thing about these emotional states is that we don't always need a reason to experience them. Often we don't know why we are feeling anxious, stressed, sad or depressed, and this can simply amplify the distress. It can also make others less supportive or tolerant. You may have heard statements (or said them to yourself) such as, "What have they got to be depressed or sad about? They have a lovely life, they don't realise how lucky they are…" etc. It's so easy to look in from the outside and pass judgement on what's visible to the outside world, without having any clue about how a person is really feeling inside. Whether we have the trappings of a "good life" or not doesn't seem to make that much difference. We feel what we feel and the first step towards changing that is simply to accept it. Don't make it wrong, don't make it right – just accept it. These emotions don't play favourites. The professional footballer making hundreds of thousands a week is just as likely to experience these states as the single parent looking for work.

Of course, when we are on the outside of these emotions, the solution, or what someone "need to do", seems simple and obvious. "Oh, you know what your problem is? You need a job" or "You just need something to take your mind off things" or the very British response, "Just pull yourself together!" What those on the outside don't realise, or are too insensitive to appreciate, is that when it's you who is in this state, your capacity to think, create or even make simple decisions is significantly impaired. That's part of the problem! These emotions are physiological. In other words, they are created by our internal biology which influences our internal system. There is an internal chemical signature to these emotional states – they are not just made up in someone's mind. These chemical signatures literally shut down or limit communication signals from the body to the brain, so our brain capacity literally shrinks. If you've ever been really scared or shocked in some way, you literally lose the ability to think. It's the weirdest experience, but it's an evolutionary glitch that essentially shuts down all non-essential internal systems to ready the body for fight, flight or freeze. The problem is that because of the stresses of modern life, we are essentially living in fight, flight or freeze mode, which doesn't give us full access to our cognitive capacity – which is exactly what we need if we are to navigate our way out!

First Steps Toward Change

Recognising and being open about how you feel is a big step forward. So too is the understanding that what you are dealing with is not some sort of personal failing – it's evolutionary biology. Thankfully, there are a number of simple things you can do to help, including paying attention to what does and does not help and doing more and less of those things respectively.

These emotions, whist all profoundly negative, are different, so I'll explore each group separately.

Anxiety/Stress

Stress and anxiety has a similar effect on our brain as a threatening experience or situation.

Just imagine if you were out walking and came face to face with a large brown bear. Your physiology would react to get you out of danger before your cognitive mind even registered that you were looking at a bear!

When we are scared, this triggers three different responses – fight, flight or freeze. These are manifest by the release of different hormones. Adrenalin, or epinephrine as it's known in the US, triggers the flight mechanism – it provides a jolt of energy so we can run away and escape danger. Noradrenaline creates the fight response, as we ready ourselves for battle. When we freeze, this is due to the release of acetylcholine. This is the "play dead" approach to danger, useful for possums but not terribly helpful for humans! These, and other hormones, literally alter our physiology and alert us to danger.

The same biological effect occurs when we are anxious, highly stressed or having a panic attack. Your body is also flooded with cortisol – the stress hormone. Remember, elevated cortisol levels have been linked to a variety of serious health problems such as obesity, diabetes, high blood pressure, heart disease, cancer, depression and dementia. It's therefore really important for our physical and mental health to keep a lid on the cortisol levels in our body.

When we are anxious or stressed, blood is often diverted to our limbs ready for action, which means that it's diverted away from our brain, which is actually the bit we need blood to get to so that we can make better decisions. This chemical and physical reaction isn't something we can manage in the moment – the computer part of our brain takes over for us and "acts" accordingly.

Unfortunately, this physiological reaction is triggered whether we are upset with our boss or we've just met a brown bear! What makes things even more complicated is that our brain can't tell the difference between something real and something vividly imagined. This is why it can be so destructive re-living old stories from the past or making up new potential disasters in the future that keep us stuck in a stressful "now". Our body doesn't know that those things aren't actually happening right now and releases the appropriate fight, flight or freeze hormone on top of buckets of cortisol that is literally making us sick and tired from the inside.

People who suffer from anxiety or stress tend to always be on high alert. Their body is always in "emergency mode" or getting ready for an emergency, and that in itself is tiring. It's also very destructive to their physical system. Interestingly, women are twice as likely to suffer from anxiety as men. This may be linked to lack of confidence, which women often suffer from more than men (especially in the workplace). Or it could simply be that men call what they are experiencing stress, rather than anxiety, because it's more socially acceptable. Most of us are not very discerning about our use of emotional labels. Even though there are 34,000 different emotions, most of us would find it difficult to name 20 and would probably struggle to identify 10 that we feel on a regular basis. It's not unlikely, therefore, that we might identify anxiety as stress or the other way around.

Either way, in a world that increasingly values style over substance, we are encouraged towards perfection. Of course, this is impossible, so we present an illusion of perfection instead, played out via social media. Social media platforms such as Facebook, Instagram and Twitter have taken "keeping up with the Jones'" to a whole new level that is simply amplifying our anxiety and stress levels still further. As the gap between reality and real life gets wider, and our need to meet some self-imposed image of perfection becomes more intense, so too does our anxiety and stress. And frankly, that just seems a little bonkers!

Beware the chameleon! **Everyone needs to learn how to adapt to those around them, so they can get on with others and get ahead in life, BUT there is a huge difference between being aware of others and adapting and being a chameleon. The chameleon will change who they are to suit what they believe others want. Trying to be anything other than who you really are is exhausting, and it certainly won't make you happy. Be your authentic self. I promise you, it's good enough. You won't be everyone's best friend, but so what? Accepting that life should be any other way is a recipe for disaster and constant disappointment. Don't try to be someone you are not, it's too tiring. Make sure you love yourself for being you and, more importantly, when you find the lucky "other", make sure they love you for exactly who you are – your authentic self.**

*To be yourself in a world that is constantly trying
to make you something else is the greatest accomplishment.*

–Ralph Waldo Emerson

Sadness/Depression

Life would be great without experiencing sadness or depression. But it's just not possible. As many scholars say, we can't experience true happiness if we don't ever experience sadness – that's what makes happiness so great. Most people experience these emotions at some point in their life, usually triggered by a situation, incident or experience. People are usually sad or depressed "about something", and it's a normal human emotion that we need to process to make sense of the world.

Sometimes we can just wake up feeling a bit sad. This may be caused by hormones, stress, or we could quite easily create sadness if we visit one of our past or future stories. Sometimes there may be no discernible reason for it at all. For the most part, sadness is a phase, it's not a permanent state. It can be distressing, but it's usually a tentatively peaceful state where we are often reflective and thoughtful.

If this state has come about from something more serious or longer lasting you may try forcing yourself to think about the positives of the situation, or at the end of the day think of three things that you experienced in your day that made you happy or you are grateful for. This will not only help you shift your mood, but also help put things into perspective and change your internal physiology for the better.

Remember, the mind and body are intrinsically connected, so if you want to change how you feel you can either change your thoughts, which will change your physiology, or you can change your physiology (e.g go for a walk, etc.) which will change your state of mind and thoughts.

When sadness doesn't pass, and becomes deeper and more permanent, it's likely to be depression. Depression used to be something no one really talked about or admitted to. Having a mental health issue of any kind was hard enough to discuss with a doctor, never mind anyone else. For too long there was a stigma of failure or weakness attached to depression and far too much unwanted and frankly stupid advice such as "Buck up."

Fortunately, times have changed, and whilst it's still challenging, our approach and acceptance of mental health issues and depression has come a long way. Unlike anxiety, stress and sadness, long term depression is not a "normal" state for us to experience indefinitely. Following a deeply traumatic life event or loss it can be almost impossible to avoid depression, but even that darkness does pass.

The good news is that it can be managed and there are some wonderful doctors and therapists who can help you manage it. So how might you recognise it and how is it different from being just sad?

Here are some ways to recognise symptoms:

How you might feel	How you might behave
• down, upset or tearful	• avoiding social events and activities you usually enjoy
• restless, agitated or irritable	
• guilty, worthless and down on yourself	• self-harming or suicidal behaviour
• empty and numb	• finding it difficult to speak or think clearly
• isolated and unable to relate to other people	• losing interest in sex
• finding no pleasure in life or things you usually enjoy	• difficulty in remembering or concentrating on things
• a sense of unreality	• using more tobacco, alcohol or other drugs than usual
• no self-confidence or self-esteem	• difficulty sleeping, or sleeping too much
• hopeless and despairing	• feeling tired all the time
• suicidal	• no appetite and losing weight, or eating too much and gaining weight
	• physical aches and pains with no obvious physical cause
	• moving very slowly, or being restless and agitated

*Symptoms taken from the mental health charity MIND

If you suffer from some or all of these symptoms, it doesn't automatically mean you are depressed. However, it's always worth seeing your doctor and getting checked out. My guess is that if this is you, not much can be worse than how you are feeling right now, so making an appointment to discuss how you feel with your doctor is a positive, proactive step. I know this can be hard. I went through a phase of depression when my dad died and I was also going through a divorce. I was at my all-time lowest point and the very thought of having to go to the doctor felt like just another failure. However, I went and cried through the whole appointment. I still felt like a failure, but I also got help. You have to be brave and know when to ask for help. It takes a little courage, but it's always worth it.

Recognising that you need help is absolutely crucial to your recovery. And let's face it, if you had a physical injury or condition you wouldn't hesitate in making an appointment with a health professional, so why should your feelings and mental health be any different from your physical health?

Beware medication too soon for too long. **My only advice would be to try the various tips and strategies before you plump for anti-depression medication. It's worth a try and sometimes little shifts can make a big difference. If they don't make enough of a difference, then certainly explore medication, but be sure to approach it as a short-term solution to help you get back on an even keel, not a long-term fix.**

Tips and Strategies

If you want to conquer the anxiety
[stress, sadness or depression] of life,
live in the moment, live in the breath.

–Amit Ray

Emotion is simply energy in motion – it's a physiological storm of some sort occurring inside your body. When we experience strong emotions, especially negative emotions, it can be tempting to squash them down, ignore them, or medicate them away with prescription drugs or a glass of wine or three. But actually, the best approach is to stay with the emotion and allow the storm to pass or move through your system. It may not always be pleasant, but if we stay with it, it naturally peters out and we emerge to survey the damage. There is an adage in personal development: "the only way out is through" – that is definitely good advice when it comes to our emotional flexibility. The only way out of sadness is through sadness. Let yourself experience it and once you do it will ease and you can move on. Although depression can be more complex, the same is true for anxiety and stress.

Below are some tips and strategies that may help you to manage these negative emotions constructively, so you can get back in the present stream of life.

• **Our story is not necessarily reality.** Remember, a great deal of what we experience is directed by the stories we make up around what events, situations or interactions mean, often drawing parallels from the past or jumping into the future to "confirm" our fabricated hypothesis. These stories are rarely objective truth and yet they are the source of our anxiety, stress, sadness or depression. Become a private detective in your own life and actively interrogate and cross-examine your stories to ascertain how much of the substance of these stories are real and how much is fiction, assumption or guesswork. Use what you discover to reassess your emotional reaction. Is it possible, for example, to turn your anxiety or sadness down a notch or two as a result of what you've discovered? Emotions are not on/off phenomena, so anything you can do to reduce the intensity will help.

- **Give yourself a deadline!** I find giving myself a sadness time limit very helpful. Try it. Next time you are sad, acknowledge that you are feeling sad and give yourself permission to feel that feeling for a specific length of time – perhaps 30 minutes, an hour, or even for the day if you are really struggling with a particular situation. After that you need to get back into action. This allows you to acknowledge your emotions and feel them properly, but stops the sadness gathering momentum and keeping you stuck in that sad place.

- **Get into healthy psychological habits**. Just as we exercise our body we must learn to manage and exercise our brain. Becoming mentally resilient and being able to question our "stories" and our beliefs will help reduce the noise and drama.

- **Get into healthy physiological habits** too. One of the easiest and quickest ways to alter how you feel is to move your body. Go for a walk, if possible into a local park or into nature. Physical movement, especially if you have to exert yourself a little, will change the chemicals circulating in your body which can lift mood. So, turn off the TV, borrow your neighbour's dog and go for a brisk walk instead.

- **Meditation is a wonderful tool for bringing you back into the present** – here and now. Even 10 minutes a day can help keep you grounded. Being in the moment, living life as it happens, is a much healthier place to be. Thinking or reliving the past or imagining the future isn't always helpful.

- **Avoid extra stress and anxiety.** Remember, when you are stressed or anxious your ability to cope with other challenges or adversity will be reduced. Avoid taking on "extra" stress or other people's worries when you are in this place. Give yourself permission to help yourself and regroup before you get back into "helping others" mode. Remember what air stewards tell you on an aeroplane: if there is a problem, fit your own oxygen mask before helping others.

- **Don't ruminate over negative story loops in your mind** – they are unhelpful and destructive. All they do is increase your anxiety and stress. If you find yourself doing this, take a 2-minute break to distract yourself. Use these 2 minutes to focus on something else, either outside or something that happened that is positive. Go through it in your mind with a full description of what you could hear, see, experience etc. Evidence shows that just 2 minutes of distracting your brain will help disrupt the negative rumination. This practice is a little like meditation, so it can feel odd or unnatural at first. Just stay with it. When you catch yourself re-living a negative event or situation, move your mind consciously back to something positive or neutral and focus on that. When it jumps back to the story, move your mind back to something else. Just like meditation, the more you practise this the easier and more natural it will become.

- **Think about what you are putting in your body.** The food we eat has a profound impact on how we feel. To function properly and at our best we need a certain amount of macro nutrients, such as protein and carbohydrate, but we also need a whole suite of micronutrients in the form of vitamins and minerals. Those micronutrients are best found in healthy, fresh fruit and vegetables and not processed food. Cut back on your sugar intake and avoid food with low or little nutritional value.
- **Lack of micronutrients could be impacting your emotional well-being.** A lack of zinc, for example, can cause anxiety, a lack of magnesium can cause sleep problems and insomnia. Consider getting tested to see if you are deficient in any micronutrients and make the appropriate alterations to your diet, or consider taking good quality supplements to rectify the imbalance.

The Spin / Release Technique (adjusted model by Richard Bandler)

Here is a very simple technique that you can use in times or anxiety, stress or sadness. It might look a bit weird, but it can be really helpful to release the pent-up emotions whizzing around your body.

1. Identify an unpleasant thought, feeling, emotion or physical symptom that you might be experiencing.
2. Notice the physical sensations and/or visual images associated with the problem or issue, and determine where you feel it in your body when you think about it.

3. Pull the problem/issue away from you with your hand, as though you were pulling it out your body, and visually see it in your hand or fist out in front of you. It can be in the form of an image or symbol.

4. With your hand or fist, start moving it in the way you feel it might be spinning. Is it spinning clockwise or counter-clockwise? If it appears motionless then ask yourself, if it was spinning, which direction would it be spinning in?

5. With your hand or fist replicate the spinning physically and slow down the spin until you reach a halt. Then reverse the direction of the spin, and get it going faster and faster until you are ready to release and throw it away.

6. After you have thrown away the unwanted image/feeling/emotion you may visualise a new healing image, symbol or gift that might appear in front of you.

7. Identify the positive message from the gift, feeling or image, and how it is meaningful to you.

8. Bring the gift back into your body and notice all of your new feelings and understandings.

Learn from yesterday, live for today, hope for tomorrow. The important thing is not to stop questioning.

–Albert Einstein

Additional Resources

Read: *The Mandala of Being* by Dr Richard Moss . This is an excellent book which explains that living in the present can give us respite from all the negative places we take ourselves to, which in turn create other problems for us.

Watch: *Guy Winch Ted Talk on Why we all need to practice emotional first aid.* He makes a compelling case for taking care of our emotions and our minds with the same diligence with which we take care of our bodies.

Get: The "Headspace App" from www.headspace.com for short, useful meditation sessions via your mobile phone

Support: From Advice Line for Mental Health Support

Chapter 6
How to Handle Controlling Behaviour
(Your own and other people's)

You will become as small as your controlling desire;
as great as your dominant aspiration.

–James Allen

Do you sometimes feel that no matter what you do a certain person will find fault and turn it against you? Do you feel unsure about sharing news or information with someone because you are scared of their reaction? Perhaps you already turn down opportunities to go out, see your friends, or advance your career because of the anticipated reaction of someone central to your life? Do you often feel as though you are walking on eggshells around a certain person, unsure which version of them is going to show up? Or perhaps you are the control freak in the family?! If you find you never do anything new or struggle to action new plans because you're afraid of the outcome and can't risk failure, or you actively prevent others from spreading their wings so as to keep you company, then this chapter may help you gain a new perspective.

What do you think of when you hear the word "control"? There are many forms and much of this book is centred on how to take positive control of your own life so you can make better, more conscious choices that move you closer to what you want and away from what you don't. Some control is necessary because it allows us to achieve what we set out to, and to predict the outcome of certain actions. This level of certainty that exerting control can bring often feels comfortable and safe. As human beings, we need to feel as though our input matters and we have a say in our own lives. It is an essential component of happiness.

But too much control can be a major challenge. And this is true whether you are the person in a controlling relationship or the person doing the controlling. People can be controlled in all sorts of relationships, personal or professional, and it's not gender specific. It's just as common to find controlling women as it is to find controlling men. Both are just as good at exerting their power to influence or direct people's behaviour or the course of events.

So, what happens if we live or work with someone who directly influences or even manipulates us in order to retain control? Would we even recognise this behaviour if it was happening to us? In some cases, this type of manipulation and control has been happening for so long that the person affected just thinks it's normal. Or perhaps they realise something isn't quite right, but have no idea how to escape from it. If you are unsure if this chapter relates to you, then consider the following scenarios…

- Is there someone in your life who believes they always know better than you do and who has a constant expectation that you will follow their instructions or wishes?
- If you don't agree with that person, they are quick to get angry or point out how foolish or stupid you must be, and that "you" are often the biggest problem in the equation.
- Perhaps you've stopped speaking up altogether because you know you will be "shot down"?
- Is that person quick to blame you and others if things don't go well, often being verbally derogatory in the process? Do they rarely, if ever, take the blame or responsibility themselves?
- Does this person always expect you to change your plans to accommodate them? Do you ever think that they seem to think your life revolves entirely around their needs and desires?
- Is there someone in your life who always insists on knowing the ins and outs of who you are with and what you are doing – usually so they can exert control over those activities? (They will usually have strong opinions about situations and people that you know and be only too happy to share them with you).
- Does this person dislike you spending time with other people who can influence your thinking? (This is often

threatening to a controlling person, because they don't want anyone influencing you except them. In response to this, they are likely to either run down your friend, become visibly annoyed or, in extreme situations, try to stop you spending time with that person).

- Is there someone in your life who has very inconsistent moods – especially around others? When you are with other people perhaps they are utterly charming, making you and everyone else feel wonderful, only to tear strips off you behind closed doors, crushing your independence, self-esteem, or worse, giving you the "silent treatment" as a punishment.

- Controlling people are often unable to hear the word "No". Instead, they will simply seek to wear you down with guilt and other manipulative strategies until you say "Yes" in order to conform with what they want.

- Do you know someone who will often pre-judge or predict a negative outcome to good news? It doesn't matter who else achieves anything or hears some welcome news, this person will always pour cold water on it and seek to trivialise or minimise the news or success. They always seek to make themselves look good at everyone else's expense.

- Perhaps you know someone who has to be right or win at all costs, even lying in order to gain ground?

- Do you know someone who controls your personal finances or seeks to control you through access to money? Do they decide who you can see and when? Or perhaps they even have a say in what you wear?

This level of control can very quickly feel stifling and these are just some of the hallmarks of abusive relationships.

It can be exhausting living or working with someone who exerts endless control over us. In my work, I often hear clients say things like, "I know they are quite controlling, but…" or "It's just easier to do it…" or "I haven't got the energy to keep fighting it…" Often these people have been in controlling relationships for so long, they don't know any different. It breaks my heart. A true friendship or relationship of any kind is a sharing balance between two people who have an equal say. It is not an invitation for one to control or manipulate the other. And such behaviour is certainly never genuine love or care.

Unfortunately, it's hard to escape a controller, but it is possible. Verbal abuse and excessive control can be just as damaging as physical abuse. In many ways, it's even harder to escape, because the bruises are on the inside and the constant control eats away at our inner resolve and courage. Abuse of any type leads to fear and so we live a half-life or mediocre life whilst we are in stuck in the controlling situation.

What is it that turns someone into a "controlling person"? The truth is, we all have the capability and we all need to exert some control over our lives, but when that spills over into controlling over people's lives, or we live less expansive and open lives as a result of our need for control, then something has to give.

When my first marriage ended, I was a single parent for five years and I was the only financial provider for my children. Needless to say, my need to control my finances and drive towards financial stability was critical. Anything that "rocked our financial boat" made me nervous and anxious. I had often thought about becoming an independent consultant and leaving the nine to five grind, but I repeatedly dismissed it as impossible because of my concern for financial stability. When I met my current husband, he encouraged me to pursue my dream and step out on my own, because he could financially support us both if he needed to. Whilst most people would think this was an amazing opportunity to put my plan in action, with a bit of a safety net, I had a huge internal reaction to it. Knowing I was solely responsible for my children was oddly comforting to me, because I could control that and I could rely on myself to do what needed to be done to provide for us. I was very uncomfortable with the fact that going out on my own might require me to rely on my husband. It was really overwhelming. I found myself having mini panic attacks at the very thought of it. It took me a while to move through what I was feeling and realise that when it came to work and money I was a control freak! The very thought of letting that go was terrifying. But that was the key: "the thought of it" was not the reality of it.

Our fear of what might, could, or may happen is always so much more intense and amplified than the real outcome. Even if things don't go well, they almost never go as badly as our mental scenario planning! Fear gets in our way. It creates unnecessary and often false worry and anxiety before we've even made a decision about what to do. Jumping into the unknown and going out on my own was one of the best things I've ever done – and had I not had faith and let go of my control I would never have experienced it.

First Steps Toward Change

Understanding why people need control in the first place can help if you feel you can be a little too controlling. If you are on the receiving end of controlling behaviour it can also help to know what might be driving that behaviour, so you can handle it more efficiently. If you are the son or daughter of a controlling parent, you have almost certainly picked up some traits through conditioning. Or, if you experienced trauma or a challenging childhood, you may also be more prone to being a "controller". Often those who have been controlled become controlling. It's the same cycle that's often seen in abuse – those who are abused as children often become abusers themselves as adults. But, we can all break any cycle if we really want to.

What usually underpins controlling behaviour is:

- **Fear**. The fear of being alone, the fear of appearing weak, the fear of the unknown, the fear of looking stupid, the fear of being "found out". The possible fears driving control are endless. Often, that fear manifests as aggression, which is usually the first line of defence for someone with control issues.
- **Ego.** The need to be right all the time, The "I told you so" moments where people can diminish others whilst building themselves up. When the need to be certain and appear confident and assured is more important than anything else. Ironically, excessive displays of ego usually mask the opposite. When ego is in the driver's seat, it is almost always a position created to protect and hide a deep lack of assurance and self-confidence.

- **Perfectionism**. We often see this in a work situation in the form of micro-managing, where nothing anyone does is ever good enough. The "If you want something done right, do it yourself" philosophy is another expression of this mind-set. It can be exhausting being a perfectionist, but let's cut to the chase here – it's a total cop out. "I'm a perfectionist" is usually code for "I'm terrified of looking foolish or making a mistake, so I'll procrastinate and create nothing whilst maintaining my air of superiority around others." Ring any bells? If so, own it, and take small steps towards changing the behaviour.

- **Habit**. Exhibiting controlling behaviour and allowing yourself to be controlled can also be a result of habit. That was certainly true for me. I was a control freak around money because I'd had to be in control of the finances my entire adult life. But life moves on, I'd moved on, and I needed to embrace the new life I had and let go of some of my more irrational fears. And if I can do it, so can you. Habits can be changed or replaced with more nurturing, constructive habits.

Being in a controlling relationship can be devastating and it happens to all sorts of people. There is no stereotype. Once inside a controlling relationship it can be extremely challenging to escape – especially if the person doing the controlling is adept at manipulation and has successfully cut you off from friends and family.

If you are the one doing the controlling, abandoning that behaviour can be equally challenging and send you into a tail spin of insecurity and fear. But change is possible for both parties. Of course, some controlling people simply don't want to change. In fact, some would say they *can't* change, especially if they are on the upper scale of dominating controllers. Narcissist often fit into this category.

Narcissistic personality disorder is a mental disorder in which people have an inflated sense of their own importance, a deep need for admiration and a lack of empathy for others. Narcissistic behaviour is on the rise in the modern world, fuelled by our endless obsession with selfies and sharing every aspect of our lives in exchange for "likes". Often, someone with narcissistic tendencies can become worse in the digital world as they seek to manufacture and project a perfect version of their life, as though it were a reflection of reality. Of course, behind this mask of ultra-confidence lies a fragile ego and little self-esteem, which is ironic because the online world is brutal and these people are therefore especially vulnerable to even the slightest criticism. It is another form of cognitive dissonance: they are desperate to be liked and noticed, which makes them increasingly vulnerable to being disliked and criticised. The self-construct or illusion a narcissist creates is often more important to them than anything else, which is why they find it so hard to change. They simply don't know who they are if no one is looking at them or paying them any attention. Needless to say, anything that threatens that perfect "self-construct" will be either dismissed, ignored or aggressively defended: "Who are you to tell me…?" etc.

A controlling relationship is one of the most unhealthy, most destructive types of relationship you can have. It has many downsides, not only to your *own* health and well-being, but it can also impact your friends and family. Often they are systematically shut out of your life in an effort to further distance you from those who could provide support as you break away. In the end, both parties miss out, their respective needs and desires constantly getting in the way of a loving, reciprocal union.

Beware too much interference. You may come across people or know family members who are in a controlling relationship. Often those individuals will know that they are in that type of situation, so they will be fully armed with well-rehearsed excuses such as, "Yes, I know he/she can be like that, but I know they love me..." or "They aren't like that all the time..." There is often no point badgering them to see something they are not willing or don't want to see. Instead, let them know you are there for them and have their back, and support them to make the transition if and when they are ready.

Personally, I don't believe that kind of love is healthy. It's a "needy love" driven by fear not love. And sadly, it's often borne out of resignation, where the thought of trying to leave or escape is too hard, or the person has been so beaten down they don't think they deserve any better. If that resonates with you, I promise you, you *do deserve better.* Please get the help you need from a counsellor or therapist; they are trained to help you. People who truly love you want you to be the best you can be. They will be supportive of what you want to do and what you want to be – even if at times they don't agree with you or are scared for you. They will support you unconditionally. Everyone deserves that.

Tips and Strategies

We are who we choose to be,
nobody is going to come and save you,
you've got to save yourself.

–**Barry Manilow**

A controlling relationship, whether at home or work, is a sad and exhausting one for both parties and that's why it is so important to do something about it. The following questions might help you decide whether you should stay and seek to re-define or re-invent the relationship, or whether it's just time to go…

- What is your gut reaction to the question, "Is it time to leave?"
- How do I feel about what's right for me?
- How will I know when I've had enough?
- What would need to happen for me to be sure I should leave?
- Has it happened yet?
- Do I want to wait until it has happened?
- If I stay, would it be for the wrong reasons?
- What would or could I gain by leaving?
- What would I advise someone else in my position to do?
- In 10 or 15 years' time, looking back at my decision to stay or go, which situation would make me happier?

If you know it's time for change, then the following ideas and strategies may help you to take the baby steps towards a different relationship or exiting the relationship all together.

- **Check in on your self-esteem and confidence.** This can be undermined or bashed in a controlling relationship, so read Chapter 10. Sometimes we can feel we aren't worthy of anything different. You are!

- **Give the "controller" the option (or choice) to make a sustained change or leave.** Being on your own might feel scary, but it's better than signing up to a life that someone else is hell bent on running for you. Don't waste any more of your precious life in a situation that makes you unhappy. Sign up a family member or friend for support, you will need it.

- **Be clear about what is acceptable to you and where your boundaries are** and be strong about what you need in your relationship and how your partner can help give that to you. In some cases, you might need to suggest what they do differently. Just asking someone to stop doing something may be hard if their behaviour has become a habit and they don't know what to replace it with. For example, I might say, "Please don't choose my food for me when we go out to a restaurant. Instead, I would like to take the time to choose myself and I will tell you what I want when I've decided." Take little steps. This is especially important if your partner recognises his or her own controlling behaviour and wants to make a change too.

- **If you are the controller in the relationship, be really aware of how you control the other person.** Catch yourself in the moment and resist putting your own opinion or desires into the mix. It's OK for you not to decide everything or manage every outcome – let the other person take the wheel, even for short periods of time. It's better than not letting go at all. Really ask yourself, what is the worst that can happen if you don't control it?

- **Seek professional help to redefine the relationship** so you can both get clear on your boundaries and set out a new, clear path towards your new relationship.

- **Acknowledge that it's hard to leave a controlling person.** If it wasn't, millions of people wouldn't still be stuck in them! You are their ultimate prize and they won't let you go easily, so you need to prepare yourself for the choppy waters ahead. Get ready for a whole cycle of emotions ranging from anger, to desperation, to charm. The controller knows how to manipulate you and they will pull out every trick in their bag to keep you in the relationship. In extreme cases, this might even be to the extent of harming themselves, which is a way of shifting the responsibility so that you are the only one who can prevent it by not leaving. If this happens to you, I urge you to seek help from a therapist or counsellor. They are well experienced in this kind of relationship manipulation and you will need support and advice.

- **Don't miss out on what "might have been".** Remember, a controlling relationship impacts all areas of your life. It not only affects your day-to-day life, you are also missing out on "what might have been" or "what might have happened, if only…" The need to control the outcome or process doesn't allow us to experience any detour from that path and, as we know, it's on detours or unplanned journeys that miracles and the wonderful unexpected can happen. Find your inner courage and bravery and make the change.

- **Read Chapter 11 on bravery and courage.**
- **Read Chapter 14 on making tough decisions.**

I am no bird; and no net ensnares me:
I am a free human being with an independent will.

–Charlotte Brontë, *Jane Eyre*

Additional Resources

Watch: *Psychology of Control: A Video Study.* This presentation is about the now famous experiment conducted by Ellen Langer and Judith Roden into control and how essential it is for personal wellbeing and health.

Read: *How to Live With a Control Freak* by Barbara Baker. The author gives useful insights into how to manage a controlling relationship and do something about it.

Read: *Controlling People: How To Recognize, Understand, and Deal With People Who Try to Control You* by Patricia Evans. Learn how to "break the spell" of control. This book deals with issues big and small for those who suffer this insidious manipulation.

Chapter 7
How to Dial Down the Drama

Have you ever found yourself embellishing a situation or experience for effect? Do you tend to make a "mountain out of a molehill"? Do you always seem to be embroiled in some sort of drama, either your own or other people's? Do these situations cause you anxiety or stress or do you secretly enjoy them? Do you stew on situations, often taking the drama and adding new internal subplots to amplify the impact – even though others may think the situation hasn't upset you? If you'd like to reduce the drama in your life, then this chapter may help.

Everybody loves a good drama. It's why we watch them on TV. Millions of people are addicted to the highs and lows of soap opera storylines or the latest gripping series as the characters' lives unravel for our viewing pleasure. It's entertaining and we always want to see what happens to the people in the story.

Life can be similar. We experience the ups and downs and the good and the bad, all weaving together in the storyline of our life. We are often adept at creating drama anywhere – at home, at work, and in our relationships. We can also be very good at making a situation or event mean something else, and I'm sure we all have a friend who's particularly good at being a drama queen! They are loud, noisy, can crave attention and the worst of the worst *always* happens to *them*!

The danger with drama, or adding drama to an event or situation, is that it can have a direct impact on your mental and physical health. If we intensify or add drama our body will respond accordingly to deal with the "threat". Cortisol, the stress hormone, is released into our bodies to help us cope, increasing our blood pressure and blood sugar amongst other things. Our body will go into fight, flight or freeze mode as discussed in Chapter 5. This readies the body to deal with whatever it thinks might be coming. However, this automatic physiological response also hampers our ability to think clearly, because our body has momentarily taken over in order to protect itself. Mentally adding drama can therefore heighten a sense of panic and anxiety that can quickly cause us to lose context or perspective and amplify the drama still further.

First Steps Toward Change

In my work, I come across people who are naturally more dramatic than others, but we all have the capacity for drama. It's important to recognise where drama fits in our life and how it differs, depending on our personality type. Extroverts, those who draw their energy from other people, can be more prone to external drama and can appear "high maintenance" to others. You may hear an extrovert say how they wear their "heart on their sleeve".. This is usually an indication of the level of emotion a person will show "in the moment".

Introverts, those who draw their energy from solitude can still experience drama, but they tend to experience it internally. They are more likely to "bottle up" their emotions, which can very easily transfer into worry or anxiety.

It's important to recognise that drama is almost totally fabricated. Sure, there may be a real situation and normal emotions attached to it, but how we deal with it and whether we handle it well or escalate it into more of a problem is almost entirely down to how we think and ultimately react to it.

Think of drama creation like an internal volcano. Initially something happens: it could be an off the cuff comment from a colleague, a meeting with your boss, a bad day at the office or an argument with your partner or children. The event or situation did happen – it wasn't your imagination – but what you then do with that event *is entirely* down to your imagination. Have a look at fig. 7.1, and see how easy it is for a relatively small issue or incident to become an emotional disaster zone.

Figure 7.1: The 'My Story' Process

As we re-tell our story to other people two things can often happen: 1) validation of our story and 2) amplification of the emotions surrounding the story. Put simply, this is how the metaphorical molehill turns into a mountain.

We all have the choice and option to reduce the impact that challenging situations have on our mind and body. We also have the ability to reduce the impact drama may have on others around us.

We always have a choice about how we "rate" the drama (see "Tips and Strategies") and this rating process can help prevent our mind from racing away and inventing scenarios that don't even necessarily exist or can't be proven.

Beware of the night drama. In the wee small hours of the morning even the most trivial drama can seem insurmountable. Know that you can be at your most imaginative and creative at night, which can result in an unhelpful escalation of whatever is causing you concern. Consider your situation and what you need to do during the daylight hours. Everything always seems more manageable when the sun is shining. Never make big decisions in the middle of the night!

Tips and Strategies

> *If you bring nothing but drama to the table,*
> *don't be surprised if everyone gets up and leaves.*
>
> –Bumper sticker

Below are some tips and strategies that you can use to lower the drama in your life. They focus on what you can do in your mind to change your perspective and reduce the stress and anxiety you may feel as a result of the drama. It's also worth considering where your drama comes from. Do you have a friend who always seems to be surrounded by drama? If so, you might want to reduce your interaction with that friend a little, or get them to read this chapter and support them to dial down their own drama too.

Rate Your Drama

We might not always be in a position to "think ahead" when we react to an unfolding situation, especially when it's a surprise. We can, however, decide to reduce the on-going drama we add to the situation, so we can better manage what happens in the present.

Here are a few tips to help you reduce the drama:

- Ask yourself, "What drama rating am I going to give this situation out of 10?"

1_____10

Fairly insignificant   —   Bafta Award
                                      Winning Performance

- What kind of reaction am I going to have on top of my present feeling? Am I adding dramatic effect …
  - To re-tell a better story?
  - To ensure people have more empathy for me?
  - Because my ego is impacted or I feel bad?
  - Because I enjoy adding more to a story to create more of an impact/get attention? (to increase my sense of being a victim or a hero?)

- How calm and collected do I need to be in order to better deal with the situation I am faced with? And can I do that with a high drama rating (given that I need brain power not fight, flight or freeze power)?
- How important is this situation to me, and does adding drama help me or make matters worse, not only for me but for others as well?

Asking these questions and rating your drama can significantly decrease the drama and therefore the mental and physical reaction you experience as a result of an event or situation.

Say your boss makes a derogatory comment about your work in jest during a meeting. You're initially upset about it, but don't say anything. As soon as the meeting is over you go for lunch. As you think about what he said, you can feel yourself getting more and more upset and so you rate your drama level. In the moment, it's definitely 8/10.

As you wait for your friend to join you for lunch you realise that you're actually getting quite excited at the idea of sharing your story with your friend. You are therefore aware that there is some enjoyment to be derived from adding drama! You are also a little embarrassed because, if you're honest with yourself, you know that particular piece of work wasn't your best. It's irritated you that your boss made a comment in front of others, but actually he said it in jest and he could have taken you aside and said something a lot worse, so maybe it's not an 8/10 after all.

Considering the fact that you have another meeting with your boss later in the day, stewing on this for the next few hours is definitely not going to make that meeting go better. By the time your friend arrives for lunch you've managed to dial your drama down to a 3/10 and you don't even mention it. Instead, you enjoy your lunch and have a constructive second meeting with your boss. Had you re-lived the situation with your friend, adding endless embellishments and assumptions about what the comment meant, you would have amplified your drama, which would have made you feel worse and certainly polluted your second meeting. Why do that to yourself?

If your rating has been amped up because you feel silly or put out, then you can choose not to feel silly or put out, give the situation a different spin so as to reduce the drama, and get on with your day. Humour is great for defusing this sort of feeling.

When you are on your own, try re-playing the thing that was said that upset you in a silly voice. Imagine you have sucked on a helium balloon or you are imitating Donald Duck and repeat the words out loud. In the example above you would re-state what your boss said in the meeting using a silly voice. This easy technique can very quickly take some of the sting out the situation and make you laugh.

By going through these questions, we can consciously take back control and dial down the drama, so we can avoid any of the negative side effects like stress, anxiety, anger or worry. Remember, you always have a choice about whether or not you allow something to upset you.

If your drama ratings are still high, there are a couple of things that can help...

Did you or the other person intentionally cause upset? Knowing that you didn't mean to upset someone or create a problem can take some of the guilt out of the situation. Knowing that others didn't intent to hurt you or cause upset can also remove some of the drama.

We are each the centre of our own universe, but we are not the centre of everyone else's universe! Consider how much other people *really care* about what you may or may not have done or said, especially if you have sorted it out or apologised if necessary. We live in a very narcissistic, selfie-obsessed age, so it's easy to think people will be stewing over something the same way we are. I promise you they are not!

> *You wouldn't worry so much about what others*
> *think of you if you realised how seldom they do.*
>
> **–Eleanor Roosevelt**

Even if you have done something you regret and have genuinely created a drama, there are very few things that can't be solved, or at least helped, by a sincere apology. Say sorry, mean it and move on. Consider how long you would like to punish yourself (or others) for making a mistake. An hour? A day? A week? Never? There isn't really any difference between a week and never, so just stop blaming yourself, learn from the situation so that you don't repeat it, and get on with your life.

Breathing Technique to Calm Your Mind and Body

Learning how to calm your mind and body during times of drama can also help to reduce the negative emotions you may experience.

Often, when we are in the middle of drama we will breath shallowly from our throat, rather than breathing deeply from our diaphragm, or we may even hold our breath. Here is the simple breathing technique that I've made reference to in a number of chapters.

1. Shift your attention so that you breathe from your tummy not the top of your chest. Often when we are asked to breathe in, we will pull our stomach in on the in-breath and push it out on the out-breath. This technique does the opposite, so that as you breathe in, you push your tummy out, and when you breathe out, you pull your tummy in. This will engage the diaphragm. It may feel odd the first time you try it, because we are so used to breathing shallowly.

2. Breath in deeply through your nose. Hold it for a few seconds (up to 5 or 6 counts or whatever is comfortable) and then breathe out through your mouth. It doesn't really matter how long you breathe in, hold and breathe out for as long as it's consistent, rhythmic and comfortable.

3. You can also add a mantra to the breath which can help to quiet the mind and also facilitate rhythm. Breathe in and while you hold the breath say out loud (or think it if you are not alone), "I breathe in calm and peace." Release the breath and once you've fully exhaled say, "I breathe out relax and

release." This also helps to signal the body to relax the muscles from the top of your head to the tips of your toes. If it helps, also imagine your muscles relaxing throughout your body. Repeat this breathing exercise for a few minutes and it will help to calm your mind and body.

Also, during periods of high drama, watch what you eat and drink. It's never wise to eat too much processed, fatty or sugar-laden food, but even less so during times of stress and anxiety. And, sorry, but lay off the booze for a while – it won't help!

Not my circus. Not my monkeys.

–**Polish proverb**

Additional Resources

Watch: Watch my video on how to reduce drama

Watch: *The Drama Triangle* by Lauren Kress. Watch how you can play different roles within the drama triangle and the steps you can take to stop playing them.

Take: An evening class or free online course from somewhere like *FutureLearn*. Often, we create drama because we are bored, so explore options to entertain yourself more constructively.

Chapter 8
Dealing with Loss and Bereavement

The risk of love is loss, and the price of loss is grief.
But the pain of grief is only a shadow when compared
with the pain of never risking love.

–Hilary Stanton Zunin

Are you struggling to come to terms with the end of a relationship, whether with a lover, friend or family member? Do you sometimes feel that your life will never be the same, or as good, again because this person is no longer in your life? Do you feel weighed down by sadness or grief at the end of the relationship? Have you lost someone you care about to a serious illness or accident and can't seem to put your life back together again? If so, you are not alone. We all have to deal with loss in some form of another, but hopefully this chapter will help guide you to a brighter tomorrow.

Loss of any kind is hard. But as Stanton Zunin's quote at the start of the chapter reminds us, loss is the inevitable consequence of love. If we love, we will, at some stage experience loss. But that knowledge should never close us off to love in the future. Instead we need to embrace it as a natural part of life. There are many kinds of loss, from the estrangement of a family member to the loss of a friendship, the loss of our health, our job or financial well-being, through to the ultimate loss – the death of a loved one. We can experience similar emotional and challenging situations to one another and yet react completely differently. We are unique and the depth of our loss and the time we take to assimilate that loss and move on can vary dramatically, depending on the experience and the person.

Loss of a relationship

When a relationship ends, whether a romantic relationship or a friendship, it can feel like a bereavement. One minute that person is a constant companion on your life journey and then they are gone. It can feel like a death and be equally bruising – especially if you were not the one who chose to end the connection.

When we form attachments and connections to other people, we get used to them being in our lives. We get used to seeing them and sharing our lives with them, so when the relationship finishes or slowly disappears we can feel that loss deeply. That feeling of missing someone (or something like a job) including the connection, routine and habits we co-create can leave a huge hole in our lives we can struggle to fill. In addition, these routines and habits then act as triggers for our elevated sense of loss.

For example, if you always met your partner for dinner on a Friday night then you will be even more acutely aware of that loss on Friday nights. If you shared a love of old movies with your former friend, watching an old movie will accentuate the loss. This can be a difficult and confusing experience – especially if we don't understand why the relationship ended.

First Steps Toward Change

One of the best first steps we can take is to really consider the relationship and what actually happened, rather than the story we may have constructed for ourselves.

A good example I can give you is in one of my own friendships. On the first day of senior school we were placed in our desks in alphabetical order and I sat next to the girl who would become my best friend for seven years. We were inseparable. We even moved from our senior school to the same sixth form at another school. When I got married a year later, she was one of my bridesmaids. A year or so after I got married, we started losing touch. I reached out a number of times, but got nothing back. To this day, I don't know what happened or why she didn't want to pursue our friendship. For years, I assumed it was because of something that I did or said, but I couldn't think what. We hadn't argued or fallen out and the loss of the friendship hit me really hard.

After years of coaching clients and frankly just growing older myself I now realise this type of situation isn't rare. Often, the reason for the split or estrangement is trivial. In fact, I've lost count of the people who, when asked what went wrong in a particular relationship, will say something like, "I can't even remember why we fell out…" or "It was over something really silly."

Despite this, the loss can play on our mind for years, eating away quietly until triggered by a memory. I know that is true for me. Every now and again I would think of my friend and all the sadness would come flooding back. I would wrack my brains trying to figure out what I might have done. At this stage in my life I was perfecting the art of "guilt", so I also got to feel guilty about the loss of my best friend as well as my mum's deteriorating health.

What I now realise is that a) I'll never know what happened and that's OK and b) it was probably nothing to do with me. In chapter 2 I talked about looking at your life like chapters in a book. We go through different chapters with different characters, different situations and surroundings. Some characters run through the whole book, through many chapters, or appear in one chapter and are gone by the next. New characters exist in our future who we've not yet met.

It may be tempting, especially if we are feeling a little low, to re-connect with people from the past. With social media that is now super easy and often we are given suggestions of 'other people you may know". Each of us will react to these suggestions in a different way. Personally, I tend to believe that if I'm no longer in touch with that person there is probably a reason for it. If I wasn't that close to them in school, I probably don't need to be their friend now some twenty years later. There is no malice in it, it's just that the person probably belongs to a past chapter in my life. I'm more excited about the people I've not met yet who may become part of my present.

Of course, the characters in our book, whether family members, friends or partners, all have their own books. You will never really know how you appear in their book because it's their book and they are writing it with the experiences of their life, just as you are writing your book with the experiences of yours. You can't control or write someone else's experience of you in their book – no matter how much you want to be in it!

People come into your life for a reason, a season or a lifetime.

–**Anon**

Often when people enter our lives for a *reason* they are there to teach us something, support us through a challenging time, or guide us in some way. Once the need is met they will often disappear without any wrongdoing on either part. Or one of you may create a situation that brings the relationship to a close. Regardless of how the relationship ends, the reason has been fulfilled and their (or your) work is done.

Those who appear in a few life chapters are often in our lives for a *season*. Those people have come into your world to share, grow and learn with you. They may bring you peace, guidance, support, or make you laugh. My school friend was a godsend to me during a difficult period in my life. She was my sounding board – a position my mum couldn't occupy because of her illness. My friend was my support system and I will always be grateful that we shared a season together.

Those who enter our lives and stay for a lifetime also teach us lessons – the good and the challenging. Our job is to embrace those lessons and put what we learn in these relationships to work in all our interactions. These relationships often challenge us to be a better person and to fulfil our potential.

Take a minute to think about the loss you are feeling. Could it be that this relationship was for a reason or a season and not a lifetime?

Tips and Strategies

The most beautiful people we have known are those who have known defeat, known suffering, known struggle, known loss, and have found their way out of those depths.

–Elisabeth Kubler-Ross

If the situation or the loss is continuing to make you feel sad, or you want some resolution, here are some things that may help:

- **Decide whether you want to do something about it or not.** Often the indecision about what to do about a situation makes the loss worse and can keep you stuck in a negative limbo state. Do you need to make an approach, try to talk to them, or do you really just need to let it go? See Chapter 14 on decision making to decide if there really is a decision to make and how much you care. Be mindful of your ego though – just wanting to have the last word is not helpful. What you need is resolution or closure, endless mud-slinging and recrimination will not give you either.

- **You can't control how someone else will respond.** If you decide that you want to make an approach you need to embrace the fact that they may not respond to your request or they may not want to pursue the relationship with you. Just because you want to "talk" or rekindle the relationship, does not mean the other person will. You must accept this before making the approach. If you are ignored or rejected it will probably make you feel even worse. That said, at least you will have closure and you'll know you did everything you could to resolve the situation. Remember, you can't badger, cajole or convince someone into loving you. If the relationship is over, it's over. Accept it, move through your emotions, and move on.

- **Stay open to the outcome.** If you do make an approach and you end up getting back in touch, happy days! It may be that they re-enter your life for another reason, season or lifetime. If you have been estranged for a period of time, give yourselves some time. You are both likely to be a little different to the people you were when you knew each other before. People grow up and develop (at least they are supposed to), so you may need to get to know each other again and the relationship may not be as you remember it. Give yourselves time to readjust and be flexible around what develops.

- **Be kind.** If you experience someone trying to get in touch with you that you would prefer to leave in one of your previous life chapters, be kind and truthful. You don't need to give a detailed, "War and Peace" version of why you'd rather not get back in touch, just keep it simple. Thank them for making the effort and wish them well.

- **If you have made the decision not to pursue the relationship – make a conscious choice to let it go.** Resign your relationship or friendship to part of your history, remember the good times and archive it. You may want to try the hot air balloon technique from Chapter 3. Put your relationship and any loss or sadness you feel in the basket of the hot air balloon and let it drift away.

- **Once you've decided to let the relationship go, take practical steps to minimise the loss** so you can get back on a more even keel as quickly as possible. Delete the person's phone number from your mobile phone and remove them from any and all social media platforms you use. Don't block, delete. Whether you are trying to get over a friendship that has gone wrong or romantic break-up, if you block that person, it's too easy to unblock – especially after a couple of drinks. If you are trying to get over a sense of loss, especially in a romantic relationship, seeing what that person is doing 20 times a day on Facebook, Snapchat, Twitter or Instagram is not helpful.

- **Consider what you are making the end of relationship mean and consider revising that story if necessary**. The only thing in life we have absolute control over is our thoughts. Even when a relationship ends badly, we don't need to catastrophise it! Our lives really don't need to be a script from our favourite soap opera! You alone have the choice to make the end of your relationship mean, "OMG, I'll never find anyone I love more. He/she was The One!" Or "NEXT! I'm now one person closer to my soul mate." The first meaning will keep you stuck looking in the rear view mirror your whole life and the second will liberate you to embrace your future – whatever that may be.

Bereavement

I lost both my parents before I was 30 years old. My mum first and then my dad passed away in 2003. I still miss him every single day, but I still have wonderful memories to call on.

The important thing to remember about bereavement is that everyone deals with it in different ways. There is no right or wrong way to grieve. The strength of relationship, the amount of shared love, the circumstances of the death, personal history, life experiences with that person, and myriad other factors play their part in the grieving process, but none of them predicts the length of despair and depth of broken-heartedness we may feel. Unfortunately, some may try!

There are two types of people in the world: those who have lost someone they love and those that have not … yet. The latter are almost always the ones who will tell us how we should grieve, when we should be "getting over it" or will offer up inane platitudes about it being "for the best". Often they mean well, but feel free to ignore them and grieve in your own time and in your own way.

First Steps Toward Change

Accept that grief is like a meandering road. We don't know the journey or the final destination and we certainly don't know how long it will take to get there. Sometimes we have people who travel with us, although each person's experience of bereavement is unique. Whether alone or sharing our loss with others, losing a loved one is incredibly hard.

Considering we all know that death is inevitable, most of us are surprisingly ill-equipped to deal with it when it arrives. On top of the loss, we often struggle with "protocol". What are we meant to do after someone dies? How long are we meant to grieve for? How are we mean to behave or hold ourselves? How long are we supposed to stay single if we lose a life partner? There can be many social and individual "expectations" from family and friends that we might feel we need to follow. Of course, respecting other people's feelings, especially when they have also been impacted by the loss is important, but again remember that people deal with loss in different ways. If you have lost someone after a long illness, then you may feel that you "lost" that person months or even years before their eventual passing. It's therefore likely that you are further through the grieving process than others might imagine. Of course, you may simply be shutting yourself off from your emotions. Some will bottle up their grief and try to hide it, others will express their raw emotion all the time, and some will try and find a happy medium between the two. Bottling up or supressing our emotions can be extremely unhealthy and those emotions will almost always spill out eventually – often as anger or frustration.

Ideally, aim for some middle ground if you can. Be compassionate with yourself and others, especially if you or others are not behaving as you might expect. No one knows the full extent of how another person feels or what's going on for that person, so be kind.

⚠

Beware other people trying to cope with you and your grief. Despite all the wonderful people around you, and the support you receive from them, you may find that friends, relatives and acquaintances can say some really stupid things when you suffer a loss. Remember, this is rarely deliberate. Chances are they have never lost anyone themselves and simply don't have enough genuine understanding of what you are going through. Often they think they are helping, or they feel so uncomfortable because they don't really know what to say, so what they do end up saying comes out wrong! If this happens to you, give them the benefit of the doubt – their intentions were almost always good, although the execution was poor. Don't judge them too harshly or let it impact you negatively. Besides, once they get home and realise what they said, they will probably feel bad enough for the both of you! You know what you know about how you feel, not how you are "meant to feel", and that's all you need to know.

Tips and Strategies

Guilt is perhaps the most painful companion of death.

–Coco Chanel

There is no timeline for "feeling better". It takes as long as it takes. People talk about being able to "manage the new normal" or "feeling the pain ease slightly every day", but it's a completely unique emotional road for each of us, so do what you feel is right for you.

That said, always make sure you stay present or look to the future, rather than getting stuck in the past. Taking each day one step at a time is a powerful and practical mantra when you are dealing with loss or bereavement. Think of it like "narrowing the beam of a spotlight" – it reminds you to just focus on what you need to deal with *right now.* This in turn helps to minimise the feeling of being overwhelmed and also gives you direction in a very directionless time. The focus on *now* also helps you maintain motion, which is absolutely essential to work through the process. It also helps you avoid unhelpful thought loops about what was or what will be, that can so easily keep you stuck.

When you get stuck it's debilitating and exhausting. Life cannot continue normally and the impact on you and those around you can be significant. Be gentle with yourself but also firm. Take one day at a time and you *will* emerge from your grief as surely as night follows day. Don't over-think anything, don't berate yourself if you don't feel better in a few weeks, but at the same time don't allow yourself to wallow in the loss for years. The person you have lost would not want you to stop living. Just keep putting one foot in front of the other and a brighter day will arrive. You will always miss that person, and there will always be moments that remind you of them and re-trigger your grief, but the day will come when you can manage that sadness and still look forward to life instead of constantly looking back.

Here are some tips and strategies that might help:

- **Talking is good, share memories**, experiences and how you feel with close family and friends. This is why we have a "wake" – it allows people to come together and remember the person, share stories and experience more than just sadness at the loss of that person. Sharing in this way also helps us to re-connect to happy times, which can help the healing process. For your own sanity and peace of mind try to limit your sharing with people outside of your close circle. They won't necessarily understand your experience and it may just end up feeling uncomfortable.

- **If you find it too hard to talk about, try starting a journal and write down how you feel each day**. Express yourself fully in the pages and allow it to become a cathartic process of self-healing. Another option is to sing or paint how you feel. The key is to express yourself in whatever way helps you to come to terms with your loss and move forward with your own life.

- **It's okay to feel numb and not feel anything. Shock and disbelief can cause your brain to short-circuit for a while.** This is totally normal. Don't rush it, or force yourself to "pull yourself together". You feel what you feel, so just allow yourself to feel that emotion.

- **Don't feel you have to make decisions about things too quickly**, being active can be good, but not at the expense of your health and wellbeing.

- **Before you got to bed each night, think of three things you are grateful for**, include one from the person you lost if you want to, or just from life itself. This is a great way of regaining perspective and coming to appreciate that you still have lots to live for. In fact, this is a great technique for all of us to use, regardless of our circumstances. Psychologist Sonja Lyubomirsky found that taking the time to consciously count our blessings as little as once a week significantly increases our overall happiness and satisfaction with life.

- **If you are really struggling and can't seem to move toward then seek out specialist help.** There are some wonderful bereavement counselling groups or therapists that could help you become "unstuck".

Although no words can really help to ease the loss you bear, just know that you are very close in every thought and prayer. To live in hearts we leave behind is not to die.

–**Thomas Campbell**

Additional Resources

Read: *On Grief and Grieving: Finding the Meaning of Grief Through the Five Stages of Loss* by Elisabeth Kubler-Ross & David Kessler. Knowing where you are in the five stages of grief can be oddly comforting and act as a map to your own grief process.

Read: *The Light of the World* by Elizabeth Alexander is a compelling memoir and a deeply felt meditation on the blessings of love, family, art and community.

Visit: *Grief and Bereavement*, a great website full of helpful reading material and video clips that may help you come to terms with your loss.

Visit: *Cruse* website – a fantastic example of a charity who support people who have been impacted by bereavement. Speaking to others who have shared your experience can be comforting.

Chapter 9
Managing Divorce and Separation

She finally gave up…
she dropped the fake smile
as a tear ran down her cheek
and she whispered to herself
"I can't do this anymore."

–Unknown

Are you wrestling with your relationship, unsure if it's working anymore? Are you beyond the wrestling stage and know deep down that it's over, but can't muster the energy or courage to do anything about it? Do you find yourself looking at your partner and wondering why or how you ever got together in the first place? Like the unknown, but all too familiar person in the quote at the start of this chapter, do you constantly tell yourself, "I can't do this anymore"? Have you already tried counselling or other types of interventions and realised that it's just not working or unlikely to improve? Have you made the move and separated from your partner, but are struggling with the reality? If so, this chapter may help.

Having been through divorce myself, I can honestly say it was the lowest point in my life. Emotionally, it took me to my darkest days. Which took me by surprise, because I'd already lost both of my parents and I genuinely felt that if I could survive the loss of my mum and dad I could survive anything. But my divorce was traumatic on a whole new level.

However, I'm not alone. Most people who have experienced divorce or separation will usually admit it's one of the most painful things they have been through. And the truth is, even if we are the person doing the leaving, the pain isn't lessened, as there is always a period of emotional adjustment when a relationship ends or is nearing its end. Some lucky couples do experience something amicable, but these types of cordial separations are rare, mainly because of the heightened intensity of emotion during separation or relationship breakdown. For those leaving it can feel exhilarating and liberating one minute, and terrifying the next. Even if they are absolutely sure they are doing the right thing, most people don't enjoy the distress their actions are going to cause another person — especially when that other person is someone they used to love, or perhaps even still love – and this, naturally, can lead to feelings of guilt. For those being left it can feel devastating, as though the rug has been pulled out from under their lives. On both sides, there is also almost certainly anger and it's often that emotion that can prevent a cordial exit from a long-term relationship.

For many people the loss of control can feel very tough. And you don't have to be a "control freak" to experience this. Not having the ability to "know" what the other person is thinking, what they may have done without you knowing, or is going to do next, is one of the hardest things about this process.

Nothing prepares you for it.

Although there may be a "best way" to end a relationship well, or a step-by-step guide to help us emerge from the legal process of divorce, it's such an individually unique and painfully personal experience that I'm not sure there is a blueprint to follow which is the *best* way. Perhaps the best we can hope for is to make the journey as smooth, painless and fast as possible for everyone involved. Perhaps we can try to keep the bitterness, anger and acrimony down to a dull roar and keep reminding ourselves that it's not just us, but our friends and family who also have to experience the break-up, especially children.

Whether we are the person leaving or the person being left, once loving and happy partners can easily turn into someone neither party recognises. Often, regardless of what side we are on, we can't believe the other person could really be "like that". Often we feel duped, as though we were in a relationship with a stranger and communication can be difficult or non-existent. We feel that the person we thought we knew didn't even exist. We ourselves can turn into someone we don't recognise as hurt, betrayal, resentment or anger consumes us, invading our minds, bodies and souls. We turn into battle-ready fighters, constantly on high-alert for any signs of unfairness or antagonism. We use these moments as fuel to feed our story of why we are right and they are wrong – our old friend "confirmation bias" is constantly in play. This narrative is common, especially when we've seen a number of "red warning flags" along the way, but have refused to acknowledge them, or worse we've constantly ignored them. But often the anger we feel when a relationship breaks down is not simply anger towards our partner, it's anger at ourselves. We know in our heart that we ignored those red flags, swept them under the carpet, ignored them or justified them, certain that they either didn't matter or that we could fix them. Just as an aside, thinking we can fix them is an especially female response, whereas ignoring them is an especially male response – and neither strategy works!

All too often we behave as though we are entering a battle zone which means over the top hostility is warranted (in our minds). Arguably, in some cases, it may well feel as though it is warranted. Perhaps a partner was unfaithful or abusive? But even then, such highly charged emotional reactions are not going to help facilitate a smooth exit. We can also flip to the other extreme of being so emotionally tired and exhausted it's a struggle to even start or go through the process of what is to come.

The truth is, in many such cases, relationships have simply disintegrated or lost their way. One or both parties has changed, and this is often a normal part of human adult development. We are supposed to evolve as human beings, but when one person does and the other person doesn't and the couple want different things, there really is very little point getting upset about that. This next bit is perhaps the toughest fact to swallow: *You can't make someone love you if that love is gone.*

I have witnessed many relationships (and I include my first marriage in this statement!), where the "writing was on the wall" – often for years. Rather than deal with the issue, however, some of those people chose to search for happiness outside of their relationship, whether that was by was kissing someone they shouldn't, flirting, or indulging in a more physical experience – all of it an outlet for desire, loneliness or desperation. The question you have to ask yourself is, "Is that really who I want to be?" Besides, people always find out. Always. A couple can so easily just end up going through the motions.

Some even believe this charade is preferable to breaking up a family.

Although I totally understand the notion of staying together for the sake of the children, the truth is, it's not the divorce that screws up children, it's the way parents go about their divorce that screws up children. I have seen children scarred by divorce and I have seen children relieved by divorce. It's not the divorce that's the problem, it's the hostility and fighting that causes the damage. It's dragging children onto the battlefield that causes the issues. When people aren't authentic with themselves or with each other, people pick up on that – especially children. They may be younger and not able to articulate what isn't right, but they will know instinctively that "something doesn't feel right". The low-level stress of not being yourself or having to put on a brave face for the sake of the kids is exhausting, especially if you do it for years. Children are not stupid. They are also incredibly resilient. I honestly believe that the vast majority of children would rather their parents were divorced and happy than married and miserable.

As parents, we always want to do the best by our children and divorce is not an easy one to manage, but your children are going to blame you for stuff whether you stayed married or not. That's what children do! Whether you worked or you didn't. Whether you lived in a big house or didn't. As long as you keep the lines of communication open, remain as honest as possible and encourage your children to stay connected to both parents, then you will come out the other side. Aim for a civil relationship with your former partner to make family logistics and planning work smoothly, so that the transition is as easy as possible for the children. Remember, they are the most important people in this process, so stay mindful of what your reactions and comments are doing to them.

First Steps Toward Change

They say hate is the opposite of love. It's not. Indifference is the opposite of love. When you have no capacity to care for, listen to, understand or respond to your partner, it's time to make some decisions. If you struggle to be with your partner alone, or only go anywhere or do anything as a family unit, rather than as a couple, it's time to look at the health of the relationship. Anyone, or any situation, you are living with that only makes you sad or unhappy should be a red flag in your life. I know this is sometimes harder to admit than we would like. If you are experiencing this, I would urge you to take control and do something about it. You may be undecided if separation or divorce is the ultimate answer, but it's clear you still need to do *something*. Perhaps it's time for counselling or an open and honest discussion with your partner? If you are both committed to fighting for the relationship, then improvement is possible. But either way, if you currently feel indifferent, then action is required now. Why waste your time and the other person's time with this half-life? You and the people around you deserve more.

The first step is to therefore acknowledge that and resolve to do something about it. Often there will be a trigger point that will tip you over the edge and push you into action. Welcome this trigger. You've reached your "action point". If you haven't reached a trigger point then why wait for something unpleasant to happen in order for you to take action? I know it might feel scary and you might need to be brave, but communicating how you feel is an important first step – despite what may happen after that conversation.

Separation or divorce doesn't make you a bad person. It's not a sign of failure. People change. We want different things and head in different directions. Stuff happens that changes our perspective on life and we simply grow apart. It's OK. We don't live in the 1950s anymore! The real test of your character is not whether you have divorced or separated, but how you went about it.

Beware of your power in the balance of divorce and separation. The mother is automatically often the main person with parental responsibility, which means the father has to sometimes negotiate visitation rights. I have seen and heard about many parents who used their children as weapons to hurt their partner. Don't do it. It doesn't matter how awful you think your ex is, or how justified you think you are based on his or her behaviour, the people you hurt most with this behaviour is your children. NEVER do it. Remember, your children will not be children forever. They will find out the truth eventually and will simply resent you for it. Plus, it's just not fair on them. Whether you like it or not, your children will still love both their mum or dad, regardless of what they have done to each other (within reason). Children are very forgiving beings. Denying your children access to one of their parents is cruel, selfish and unnecessary, unless there is a very good safety reason for it. I know you might be angry, resentful and be in constant pain, but don't take it out on your children by putting them in the middle and making them choose. They don't care who did what, they just want to be loved and feel secure. So whatever you have to do in order to get that done, do it.

Tips and Strategies

Whether life finds us guilty or not guilty,
we ourselves know we are not innocent.

–Sándor Márai

Apart from the deep heartbreak and grief at the loss of a relationship (see Chapter 8), the other thing that makes it hard is the loss of control. When people split up you are no longer the unit that decides things together. You will have outside influencers telling you what you should be doing and how you have to look after yourself. You can't force your partner to do things you want or need them to do, like take the settlement, or sell the house, or sign the divorce paperwork. You can only negotiate and cajole, all at a time when the relationship and quality of communication is at an all-time low. Loss of control or the ability to force the other person to do things in order to complete or finalise the process is stressful, really stressful, and this is what makes it hard. Below are some tips and strategies to help ease the process.

- **Don't try and control everything** – it's not possible and a sure path to resentment and frustration. When this gets especially tough (say when your ex is delaying paperwork), start to plan or think about what the future might look like when everything is settled. There will be some aspects that you can control. If some things depend on an outcome you are waiting for, there is still nothing wrong with imagining what it might or could look like. Get through your present frustration by taking fantasy trips into your new, better future, and use that imagery to pull you through each day.

- **Try to prevent brain shut down**. Remember, when you are stressed, anxious tired, or all of the above and more, our brain can lose its ability to think and be rational. Use your trusted friends to help you navigate decisions, especially ones that have financial implications.

- **Make sure you are constantly looking forward and not backwards.** No amount of replaying what happened over in your mind, wondering what you could have done differently, will help you. Besides, this type of self-crucifixion only hurts you, not the other person. Feeling angry is normal, but don't let it take over (see Chapter 3 on Shifting Anger).

- **Do seek help if you need it,** there are some wonderful therapists who can help you to be more constructive around your current and future life. They can help with self-esteem and all the things that take a hit when we have to go through separation or divorce.

- **Expect change in other relationships.** A separation or divorce doesn't just impact you and your immediate family. Friendships are also likely to change. Your social circle may suddenly get smaller. Get ready for friends to decide whose side they are on. There may be some who decide not to take sides, but there are others who may never speak to you again, regardless of whether you were the "bad guy" or not. If someone was your friend before the relationship, they are likely to remain your friend after it. If someone was your ex's friend before the relationship, they are likely to stay your ex's friend after the break-up. Those friends you made as a couple are usually the tricky ones, as the couple decide who to stay in contact with. Don't take this personally. Stick close to your enduring friendships and weather the storm. You will need to have highly trusted friends around you who can help you remain constructive, but who are empathetic at the same time.

- **Where possible, don't make any big sweeping decisions**. Take one day at a time. Try to remain physically active, eat healthily and take up a hobby, if it distracts you from the reality of the situation. It will sort itself out. However painful it may feel or be right now, have faith and hope – there is always light at the end of the tunnel. Remember the sky is always darkest just before the dawn.

- **Expect tricky situations and challenging moments**. If you divorce and you have children, the next few years can be irritating as you negotiate with your ex-partner on "child expectations and duties". Depending on the ages of your children, you will probably still need to communicate with each other. Your ex may enter a new relationship. This can be especially tough if your ex initiated the divorce. You may enter a new relationship which could be challenging for your ex and your children. Wherever you can, try and pull down the "best for the children filter" with your responses and actions. Again, it will be hard, but it's a reality of divorce that we all must come to terms with, whether we like it or not. You have the ability to make it easier for yourself in the way you react and manage it. Always seek to be the "bigger person" and remember no one will ever replace you or their father in the eyes of your children.

- **Don't close yourself down.** Following a divorce, even a relatively amicable one, it's very easy to decide that you are never getting married again or to assume you'll never find anyone else. Just don't go there, there is no need. Take the time to rest, recoup and figure out who you are and what you want. The only type of relationship worth having is when both people want to be in that relationship and they love each other equally. If that isn't happening, or wasn't happening, choose instead to be grateful that one of you had the courage to bring the relationship to an end, therefore freeing you both to find happiness.

- **Don't waste your time festering over the relationship**. This can be especially difficult if your ex cheated on you, lied, or somehow betrayed you. This type of betrayal can be brutal, upsetting and heart breaking. It can shake us to our core and often we can stop trusting anyone. Our confusion can often drive us to uncover all the gory details. The urge to "know" (but the upset that comes with "knowing") is often like a bizarre form of torture. We may be incensed and plot revenge, imagining and reimagining different scenarios which enable us to be more in control and vengeful. The temptation to turn into Sherlock Holmes and investigate the crime is almost irresistible, especially with the technology available to us today that makes such an option too easily accessible. The question to consider, as you're turning your life upside down is, "What more do I really need to know?" You already know that your partner cheated on you. If that's a "deal breaker" for you, then what is more information going to provide? How much more evidence do you need? How much information is going to help you feel better? How much grilling and interrogation will make it go away? My guess is none. Instead, really think about what will benefit you and what will continue to hurt you. Choose only what is going to support you. Some couples can get over an affair and some can't. Often counselling can help. I would always advise that you start from a position of potential forgiveness and decide if you both want to repair the relationship or not. It won't be easy, but it can be done. Don't walk away until you are absolutely sure that the relationship is over.

- **Sunny times are ahead – keep the faith!** From my own personal experience of divorce, being a single parent for five years, experiencing online dating (you name it, I tried it), I can tell you that there is a sunny future out there for you. I didn't think I would ever find it, but I did, and you will too. One of the best bits of advice I was given by a friend, when I was feeling as though I was not going to meet anyone else was, "You need to find someone who allows you to be you." In other words, don't change for someone else, find someone who appreciates and loves you for who you are, warts and all! Life gives us opportunities in the strangest of ways. This could be yours.

> *The day he moved out was terrible –*
> *That evening she went through hell.*
> *His absence wasn't a problem*
> *But the corkscrew had gone as well.*

–**Wendy Cope,** *Serious Concerns*

Additional Resources

Read: *Rebuilding When Your Relationship Ends* by Dr Bruce Fisher & Dr Robert Alberti provides a proven nineteen-step process for putting your life back together after divorce.

Read: *Getting Past Your Breakup: How to Turn a Devastating Loss into the Best Thing That Ever Happened to You* by Susan J. Elliotts offers another roadmap for overcoming the painful end of any romantic relationship, even divorce.

Watch: *Breaking up Doesn't Have to Leave You Broken* by Dr Gary Lewandowski. Through his research he has found that more people experience a positive impact on their life rather than a negative one after a break-up.

Chapter 10
Improving Your Self Esteem and Confidence

The moment you doubt whether you can fly,
you cease forever to be able to do it.

–J.M. Barrie

Do you ever feel unsure of yourself? Do you feel like a failure? Do you consider yourself someone with fairly low self-esteem or someone who takes things too personally or emotionally? Do you ever wish you had more confidence? Do you put yourself down in front of others or resent other people's success? Do you often find yourself saying, "Yes" to other people's requests when you really want to say, "No"? Are you constantly worrying about something, but don't do anything to fix what you're worrying about? What would you do if you believed you could not fail? What would you try? Are there things in your life you'd like to change, or new adventures you'd like to pursue, but you're too scared to try? If so, then your self-esteem and confidence may need a boost and this chapter may help.

Self-esteem and confidence are two of the key contributing factors in actively moving toward the things we want to experience and away from the things we don't want to experience. Most people have a confidence issue in one form or another. Some may be confident about the way they look, but not confident about their intelligence, or vice versa. Others may be confident around a particular skill set, but that confidence doesn't translate to relationships or communication skills. No one is perfect, although we live in a world that tells us we should be, or expects us to be (or at least expects us to pretend to be – especially on social media!). We are reminded daily what we should and shouldn't look like and what our lives would include if we were "successful". Social media, the press and TV all provide unrealistic, imaginary benchmarks for us to judge ourselves against, every day! It used to be only women who were judged on their looks, but now men are under the same sort of pressure that women have endured for decades.

We've all met people who seem to project unshakable self-confidence, often bordering on arrogance. But have you ever stopped to ask if that confidence is real? In my experience, those who are genuinely confident have a quiet assuredness about them. They are rarely front and centre blowing their own trumpet.

When it comes to self-esteem and confidence there are some unusual paradoxes. On one hand, we are often told to behave "as if". In other words, while confidence is an internal belief about our abilities in a certain area, even if those beliefs are not rock solid we can pretend to be confident, which in turn actually makes us feel more confident. It's a physiological thing as much as a mental thing. Read Chapter 11 and the work done by Amy Cuddy that proves this mind/body connection.

You may have heard of the statement "projection is perception". In other words, what we project to the world is how other people will perceive us – whether that projection is true or not. So even if we don't feel strong and self-assured on the inside, we can demonstrate that assuredness on the outside, and as long as we don't go overboard into arrogance, can even persuade ourselves and others that we are confident, even when we are not!

However, on the flip side of this advice (hence the paradox) is something called the "imposter syndrome". If we constantly pretend to be more confident than we feel inside, but don't learn strategies to increase our genuine sense of confidence and assimilate our learning to move from "faking it" to "making it", then we can end up feeling like a fraud. It is also something experienced by high achieving individuals who are unable to internalise their accomplishments, and who live with the persistent fear of being "found out". Women are particularly adept at the imposter syndrome. Too frequently, women in highly demanding jobs believe they got there by luck, or some other kind of subterfuge, and feel they have to be as good, if not better than their male peers. However, imposter syndrome is certainly not an exclusively female issue.

Identified by clinical psychologists Dr Pauline R. Clance and Suzanne A. Imes in 1978, imposter syndrome is something I come across frequently in my coaching work. Often, people suffering from this illusion feel like they are the only ones who feel this way. They're not, it's remarkably common. It can arise when someone is promoted into a role they don't feel worthy of, or they land a job they never dreamed they would actually get, or are in a relationship with someone they believe is "out of their league". Secretly, they believe that they are not intelligent/creative/attractive/likeable (delete accordingly) enough to be in the position they find themselves in. As a result, it's only a matter of time before they get exposed, marched off the premises, or dumped for being the imposter they believe they are.

First of all, all of us feel this way from time to time. If we are learning new skills on the job or flying by the seat of our pants, it's absolutely normal to feel out of our depth. But that shouldn't stop us stepping out our comfort zone (see Chapter 11 for more on this).

If you find yourself feeling a fraud, remind yourself of the existence of the imposter syndrome and just how common it is. You are not alone! Also, take the time to remind yourself just how hard you have worked and how many times you have done a good job, been successful or helped others be successful, or how much you bring to your relationship. We don't always know what we are doing and that's fine. We still need to do new things, embark on new relationships, take new opportunities and experiment with life.

⚠

Beware of the Fear Filters. Remember we are very good at placing "filters" over what we see and believe about ourselves. We can adjust reality to make it suit our story (usually in a negative fashion) and our purpose. Fear of failure can lead us down a path of never trying anything, just in case we fail at it. More importantly, if we do try and we fail, it can make us never try again. Everyone fails at something. Many try again and get a better outcome. Don't let failure stand in your way or allow it to tell you that you are less than you are or could be.

First Steps Toward Change

Over the years, I've learnt that self-esteem and confidence come and go. It doesn't seem to be an exact science. How we grow up, how we are parented, our life experiences and how we develop as adults – all this feeds into our self-esteem and confidence. Our online world also adds additional pressure, especially to children and young adults who don't know a world without the pressure of maintaining an online presence and its obsession with perfection, the number of "likes" we get, and an abundance of narcissistic selfies.

Often our innate child-like confidence is simply knocked out of us by life and other people. It sounds brutal, and a perfect opportunity for us to blame our parents and society for our misfortunes, but this process is actually pretty universal. People can often be very cruel to each other and do and say things that can have a profound impact on a young mind. Ironically, many are driven by love and a desire to keep us from danger. Parents may, for example, relentlessly remind their daughter of "stranger danger", telling horror story after horror story to ensure she gets the message and stays safe. Take this too far, however, and its reiteration can make the daughter extremely shy and reserved, which carries forward into adulthood. Of course, we are also impacted by people who don't have our best interests at heart and are just mean and bitter, hell bent on passing on that bitterness. In those situations, it's worth remembering that "projection is perception". All those horrible things that someone is saying to you are often simply a reflection of who they are, not who you are.

Regardless of how they are created, what we are repeatedly told or experience when we are young creates our beliefs about the world. The positive beliefs such as, "I'm good at maths" or "I'm smart" can help direct us toward additional positive experiences, open up opportunities, and help us develop as adult human beings. The negative ones, often known as "limiting beliefs" can and do hold us back. Limiting beliefs can be what we think about ourselves and what we think we are capable of. They include things like, "I'm not good with people" or "I'm not smart" or 'I don't deserve to be happy" – the list is endless. Rather unsurprisingly, limiting beliefs have a profound influence on what we expect from ourselves and others, which in turn alters the outcome and impacts the "reality" we create for ourselves in something called the "Pygmalion Effect".

Harvard social psychologist, Dr Robert Rosenthal, and Lenore Jacobson wrote about the Pygmalion Effect which is illustrated in figure 10.1. Essentially, their theory is based on "self-fulfilling prophecies". In other words, "we get what we expect".

Figure 10.1: Pygmalion Effect

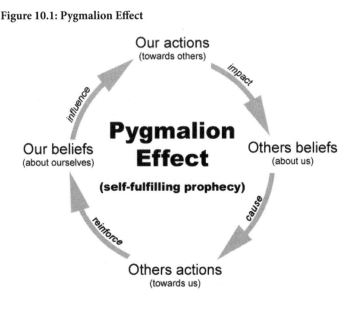

The name "Pygmalion Effect" is taken from a play by George Bernard Shaw where a professor makes a bet that he can teach a flower girl how to behave like a lady. You might recognise the plot, it was used again in the 1980s movie *Trading Places* with Eddie Murphy and Dan Aykroyd.

To illustrate the real impact of expectations, Rosenthal conducted an experiment called *Pygmalion in the Classroom*. He tested 18 classes of elementary school students using non-verbal intelligence tests and identified 20 per cent of those students as being "intellectual bloomers". The teachers of these bloomers were then informed and told that they could expect to see significant intellectual gains from those kids.

Of course, the teachers assumed this identification was based on test results, but actually the bloomers were chosen randomly. Eight months later all the kids were re-tested and those identified as bloomers *had* actually increased in IQ points over the rest of the group.

The expectation of improvement set in motion the chain of events shown in Figure 10.1.

Essentially, the teachers in Rosenthal's experiment immediately formed expectations of ability and intelligence based on what they were told and those expectations changed their behaviour and reinforced their beliefs about each child.

If the teacher believed they were teaching a "bloomer", they were much more likely to spend extra time with that child. They were more likely to make a special effort to ensure those children were supported and understood the material. They were more likely to encourage those kids to work hard, so as to allow their intelligence to flourish. On the flip side, if a "bloomer" made a mistake or was disruptive in class, they were much more likely to put that down to the student having a lapse of concentration or an "off day". The teacher's expectations of that child would therefore massively influence their day to day interactions.

If the teacher believed they were interacting with a non-bloomer, they were much less likely to spend time with that child. If a non-bloomer made a mistake there would be little extra help. After all, that child had average intellectual capabilities, so why waste time fostering something that just wasn't there?! If the non-bloomer was disruptive it would be put down to their averageness. The teachers were less patient, less encouraging and naturally favoured the bloomers because their input would be more likely to bear fruit. Of course, if a non-bloomer did well in a test or produced a good piece of work, the teacher was more suspicious of their effort or simply put it down to luck!

The only difference between those who improved their IQ score and those who didn't was the teacher's expectations of that improvement. Just think about that for a moment. What changed for those kids whose IQ increased? The only thing that changed was their teachers' behaviour towards them. They were encouraged and supported and therefore their self-esteem and confidence were bolstered, which also undoubtedly increased their effort and sense of wellbeing.

No doubt, the teachers considered the outcome of the tests as validation for their efforts. Until, of course, Dr Rosenthal revealed the *real* experiment – to test just how much teachers' expectations about the potential of each child influenced the potential of each child! It's a sobering thought and something that we should all remember: people will always rise or fall to meet our expectations!

This is why fostering self-esteem and confidence is so important. We experience what we expect. The more we believe something, whether good or bad, the more likely we are to make that belief or expectation a reality. There is no such thing as luck – the more open we are towards positive action and opportunity, the more positive action and opportunity will come our way. And, this magnetic pull between what we believe and what we experience works equally well for good and bad expectations, so focus on the upside, the positive opportunity, and what you want to achieve, not what you want to get away from.

Tips and Strategies

Optimism is the faith that leads to achievement.
Nothing can be done without hope and confidence.

–Helen Keller

Self-esteem and confidence are simply states of mind. We can use a variety of techniques to change our state of mind and access better, more constructive resources when we need them.

The Three Mentors

This first exercise can actually be used for all sorts of positive resources that you may need access to. It can help you to gain a new perspective on the situation or circumstance via your "three mentors", which can help you to generate the emotional state you need – whether that is self-esteem, confidence, bravery or courage etc.

Imagine you have three mentors. Some prefer the term :Guardian Angels", but either is fine, whatever feels best to you. These individuals can be people you know and respect personally, or they can be fictional individuals who embody certain traits, or they can be people you admire but may never have met or known personally, such as Nelson Mandela or the Dalai Lama, for instance. Choose people who you imagine would know what to do in your particular situation. For example, if you were having problems in your business and needed to be confident, you may select Sir Richard Branson as your mentor, as he knows a thing or two about self-confidence. If you need to deal with a health issue, choose a mentor who is a shining example of health and vitality, or someone who you believe knows a lot about your condition.

I often use my dad for this exercise. Sadly, he died in 2003, but I still "consult" him on various things where I need his advice. This may seem strange, but when you know someone as well as I knew Dad, or know the "myth" around a certain personality, it's amazing how easy the advice arrives from that other person.

Napoleon Hill, author of the famous self-help book *Think and Grow Rich* talks of this idea of consulting "invisible counsellors". Hill was placed in the unusual position of being asked to study success by Andrew Carnegie and was given unprecedented access to the movers and shakers of the day, including Teddy Roosevelt, Henry Ford and JD Rockefeller. He learned a great deal over the course of 25 year's study. Towards the end of his book he talks about the sixth sense and how we can access "infinite intelligence" through this technique. He even states, "On scores of occasions when I have faced emergencies, some of them so grave that my life was in jeopardy, I have been miraculously guided past these difficulties through the influence of my 'invisible counsellors'."

Whether you believe in this idea or not doesn't really matter, try the technique if you are struggling to muster the self-esteem and confidence you need. Choose mentors who might be famous for their confidence, or who you trust implicitly, and ask them for their advice. It doesn't matter if they are relatives or people you have seen in a film – do whatever works for you. Using your imagination in this way forces you to shift your perspective and you may just come up with some useful insights.

At its simplest and perhaps least esoteric, all this technique does is allow you to stand in someone else's shoes for a moment and from that vantage point you may see a way forward that you couldn't see before. It can be a really powerful and easy way to get past our own negativity and fear.

1. Get yourself in a calm, relaxing place.
2. Think of a challenging situation or a change that you want to make in your life. Imagine a circle on the floor, just in front of you.
3. Now think of three people, animals, or beings (guardian angels etc.) that love you or you've called upon to support you in your endeavours.
4. Have them all stand next to you so you leave the circle in front of you empty.
5. Imagine yourself stepping "into" the first mentor and view yourself. What words of support would the mentor say to you? What resources does that mentor have that they could share with you to help you?
6. Now step into the circle and bring your mentor with you, along with their words of wisdom and resources.
7. Repeat steps 5 & 6 with your other two mentors.
8. Once you've finished the process your circle will be full of

messages of support and internal resources, such as self-esteem and confidence, that you are "channelling" from your mentors. If it helps, you can imagine them placing their hands on your shoulders as an expression of unity and strength.

9. Now think about your challenge or the thing you want to change. Feel the strength and the resources you now have to face this challenge. Hopefully you will feel different – more robust and ready to go!

10. The great thing about this exercise is that you can use it whenever you need to – you don't have to go through all the steps, but you can imagine and call in your mentor or mentors when you need them, to help you grow your own resources!

Below are some other ideas, tips and strategies to help you increase your self-esteem and confidence:

- **Knowing what you don't want can help**. I have lost count of the people I coach who say, "I don't really know what I want, but I know I don't want this." Often they feel silly, but actually it's a really great start! Sometimes you have to figure out what you don't want and what you don't like before you can start creating or imagining what you do want. Take some time to reflect on your life and consider where you lose the most confidence. Is there some part of your life that is causing you the most anguish? If so, identify it and focus your energy on removing that hurdle from your life, whether that's a toxic partner who is constantly running you down, part of your job that you feel ill-equipped to do, or simply poor skin! My friend's daughter was really struggling with her skin and it was seriously knocking her confidence. What made it worse was that it was a new phenomenon – she'd never had poor skin in her teens. It turned out that as a student, she was eating too much cheese! Someone suggested she may be lactose intolerant, so she cut out dairy from her diet and her skin cleared up in a matter of weeks. Take the time to identify what is causing you upset or knocking your confidence and see if you can find a solution. Some things might be easier to fix or solve than you think and it will make you much more open to figuring out all the things you do want in your life. Your self-esteem and confidence will go from strength to strength.

- **Be aware of people around you who bolster or diminish your self-esteem and confidence** (see Chapter 6 on Control). Surround yourself with people who appreciate your gifts instead of pointing out your weaknesses. We all have a unique combination of strengths and weaknesses that we utilise in our lives. We will never turn our weaknesses into strengths. If weaknesses are holding us back, we can improve them a little, so that they stop being a handicap to us, but after that we need to focus on our strengths. Embrace them. They are what will amplify your self-esteem and self-confidence.

- **Really think about what you are good at, embrace those gifts and appreciate them**. If you can't think of anything, think back to a time when you were in control, confident and you sorted something out. What was it that helped you? Resilience? Being organised? Being passionate? If you take the time to reflect you will come up with some resources that you can conjure up again when you need them.

- **If you're unsure what your gifts are, go hunting**. If you really can't think of anything, then try investing in a personality profiling tool. There are many tools available online. One that is particularly useful and easy to understand is the Clifton StrengthFinder, created by Donald O. Clifton, a man considered to be the "father of strengths-based psychology". In the late 1990s, as the field of positive psychology gathered pace, it became clearer that focusing on weaknesses and seeking to "fix" them was a pointless and soul destroying waste of time and money. Based on a 40 year Gallup study of human strengths Clifton identified 34 of the most common talents and developed an assessment tool to help people discover and understand those talents, so they were better able to find their fit.

- **Think of your body and mind holistically** – both need to be looked after in order for you to be able to operate at your best. Consider what you eat and drink and how your fuel may be impacting your mental, as well as physical health. This is not just about steering clear of fats, sugar or processed food and alcohol – there is now a mountain of research that links deficiencies in certain nutrients to all sorts of mental health issues from anxiety, to insomnia to depression. Some of the things you can do to get your holistic self into a better place include:

  - **Eating healthily** – that doesn't just mean more fruit and vegetables, it means more organic or traditionally produced fruits and vegetables that are higher in micronutrients, lower in, or free from, pesticides and chemical fertilisers, and not wrapped in plastic, as well as good quality, traditionally reared meat. Remember, you really are what you eat!

  - **Getting enough sleep** (you can use the breathing

technique in Chapter 7 to aid sleep). If you struggle with sleep, consider getting your micronutrient levels measured. You could be deficient in zinc or magnesium.

- **Exercise.** Even some gardening or walking is better than nothing – anything that connects you to the outside world and requires you to use your body is going to help boost your self-esteem and confidence.

- **Don't try to keep up with others** or compare yourself to others. If we look, we can all find some element of our body, brain or life we wish we could change – better hair, longer legs, a more "academic" brain, the list can be endless. It's easy to look at others and compare; to think they have it better than we do. We mistakenly believe that if only we had X, Y and Z our life would be perfect. It wouldn't. You would just start the comparison at a different level. At the age of 45 I decided my face was starting to go south, and I have friends of a similar age who seem to be holding time back, and even a few who are starting to look younger! Of course, this just amplifies my fear that I need to do something. I know some of my friends are getting artificial help, but I quite like my eyebrows where they are and don't want to look constantly surprised! BUT, I still catch myself comparing. For some people, how they look is a real emotional challenge and it can be exhausting. No amount of magazine articles saying "love what you have" is going to make them feel better. If you find this happening to you, I would urge you to do what I do and broaden out who you are. In other words, consider all that you are, do, have achieved and not just what you look like. What do your friends appreciate about you? What does your partner love about you? What are you passionate about? Life is so much more than one dimension – whether that is looks, brains or achievements etc. Resist the temptation to compare yourself to others, especially airbrushed celebrities and models. Even *they* don't look like that in real life!

- Failing that, I would urge you to seek help. Self-esteem in regard to your appearance can run deep for all sorts of reasons, but there are people who can help you. Don't waste any more time being in a place that makes you unhappy. What do you really have to lose?

- Those of us who struggle with low self-esteem or confidence tend to be negative about outcomes before we have even experienced them. This may seem like a sensible strategy, because we can manage expectations for ourselves and others, but remember the Pygmalion Effect. We get what we expect. Catch yourself when you do this. Accept that things will be what they will be, regardless of how much we try to anticipate the outcome. Besides, sometimes not getting the outcome we wanted or getting the outcome we dreaded, might just be the right thing for us at that time. Most of us give the best we have at the time, and that's all we can really ask for – regardless of the outcome!

- Look after *you*. Create your own pace. Don't try and stuff a thousand things into one day. Being busy can often be a tactic we employ to avoid facing our issues. When we try to do too much it can impact our self-esteem as we rarely do everything well if we are struggling to find the time. Prioritise and take time out to do nothing and just chill.

- Do something for yourself that you are passionate about

and that gives you inner strength. It could be baking, walking in the countryside – it doesn't have to be earth shattering, just something that you love to do. Do it more often.

Start making small steps today, even if they seem insignificant. Do something that moves you towards improved self-esteem and greater confidence. It's worth it. If you continue to struggle, please do seek help, there are some wonderful therapists and counsellors who can help you. Today could be the first day.

Owning our story can be hard, but not nearly as difficult as spending our lives running from it. Embracing our vulnerabilities is risky, but not nearly as dangerous as giving up on love and belonging and joy—the experiences that make us the most vulnerable. Only when we are brave enough to explore the darkness will we discover the infinite power of our light.

–**Brene Brown**

Additional Resources

Read: *Boost your Self-Esteem* by John Caunt

Watch: *The Pygmalion Effect and the Power of Positive Expectations* and hear Dr Robert Rosenthal talk about the experiment above – a great reminder of the impact of expectations on outcome.

Watch: *Finding Joe* by Patrick Takaya Solomon, a film/documentary based on the work by Joseph Campbell – inspirational and worthwhile.

Chapter 11
How to be Brave or Courageous

*Courage does not always roar. Sometimes
courage is the quiet voice at the end of the day saying,
"I will try again tomorrow."*

–Mary Anne Radmacher

Do you ever read biographies of amazing people and feel in awe
of what they have done? Does that awe sometimes feel a little
despondent because you don't believe you could be so brave?
Do you ever feel that your life would be better if you could just
muster up a little more courage to pursue your dreams or exit a
poor situation? Do you feel as though there is a major decision
on your horizon, but you don't feel brave enough to make the

tough choice? Do you wonder if you've ever been brave or courageous in your whole life? If so, a little more insight into these human qualities may help you to access them.

We all have courage inside of us. It is as human as the blood that courses through our veins. Courage is like an inner reservoir we are able to draw on when we need to, although many of us only really discover our courage when we are in a tough situation or someone we love is in danger. Bravery, on the other hand is the action, behaviour or outcome of courage – it's the active facing of our fears so we can step into the unknown, or even into the known!

First Steps Toward Change

Perhaps the biggest hurdle we need to navigate in order to access our courage is the fact that we've been hoodwinked by TV, film and the media to believe that bravery and courage are only required for "big" acts – climbing mountains or rescuing small children from burning buildings. The courage and bravery we see on TV, or hear about in the nightly news, often creates an impossibly high bar that we see it as relevant to "other people" living "other lives".

The truth is much less dramatic. Anything that makes you feel slightly scared – even if it's getting a spider out the bathroom without just killing it – will require courage, especially if you hate spiders! Learning to ski in your 40s because your kids enjoyed a school trip and want to go again, requires a little courage. Depending on your personality, you may need to call on some bravery to meet new people or attend an interview.

The first time I met my friend Elaine was at an NLP Master Practitioner training program. She was telling the group about her interview phobia. This wasn't a little fear or discomfort, but a flat-out panic about interviews. She was the manager of a Supported Housing initiative. People in their early 20s who had come out of prison, but didn't have anywhere else to go, would go to the facility to help with the rehabilitation and transition back to everyday life.

Needless to say, this was a tough place and a tough job. Often the residents had serious issues ranging from mental disorders to drug and alcohol addiction. Elaine was paid £18,000 a year for that role! As part of the course we all had to introduce ourselves and say why we were at the course and Elaine explained her story to the group and said that what she really wanted to achieve from the course was the ability to earn £19,000 a year!

I remember feeling really uncomfortable about that. My background was in PR and I knew how much people her age made in that profession and it was considerably more than £19,000 a year. Her expectations were just so low, probably fuelled by her fear of interviews. She was terrified of interviews. Sometimes she physically ran out or she would clam up and she wouldn't get the job. She was on the course not only because she wanted to further her coaching and counselling skills, but she also hoped that NLP could help her get over her fear of interviewing so she could find a better job.

It worked. Although she was still scared, she was able to keep a lid on her fear for the first time and she started to set up lots of interviews just to test herself. One of the first interviews she went to was with an estate agent. Although still scared, she was able to muster her bravery and complete the interview. That experience gave her confidence and she built on that progress.

A year later she had quit her job and set up a care agency. Ironically, this involved a 6-hour interview with the Care Quality Commission (CQC). She passed with flying colours and now runs her own care agency employing over 10 staff. She's making considerably more than £19,000 a year!

I love this story because it was all made possible because Elaine recognised that her fear of interviewing was holding her back and she faced that fear head on. She had no direct experience of running a business, or the care industry, and is also dyslexic, and yet with a little effort and a dash of bravery and courage she completely changed her life.

Tips and Strategies

Leap and the net will appear.

–Julia Margaret Cameron

I was skiing recently in the Alps and was on a ski lift going up the mountain. Next to me was Frasier, who was six years old and part of a ski school. We were chatting and I said, "Frasier, if I get scared at the top of the hill what would your advice be to me?" He thought about it for a minute and turned to me and said, "Always face your fear!" Frasier was only six, but that's great advice.

Embrace the Challenge Zone

We are creatures of habit and we generally don't like change that much. Change, by definition, is moving from something that's known to something that's unknown. Most of us prefer the known because there are no surprises there – it's our comfort zone. But there is also no growth and no change in the comfort zone. If we are to harness the power of courage to face difficult situations and make constructive change, we need to be willing to move into the challenge zone (see Figure 11.1)

Figure 11.1: The Change Zone

If you are constantly in your comfort zone, how fulfilled do you feel? Sure, it's a nice safe place (some would say boring), but are you really doing what you want to do and being who you want to be if you are permanently in your comfort zone? In order to move into the next zone, we need to access the courage to push out beyond our comfort zone and into the challenge zone. But that push doesn't need to move us into the panic zone. If you are spending too much time in the panic zone, it means that you aren't in control of what you are doing, or someone else is. The panic zone is actually almost as immobilising as the comfort zone, only it's fear not comfort that's driving the bus! The key with change is incremental "stretch change" that pushes you past what's comfortable and easy, but not into overwhelm, fear and panic. Bring yourself back into what you know and/or what you need to do in order to find your own inner resources to fuel and power yourself in the challenge zone.

Embrace the challenge zone. This is where we learn, grow and develop as human beings. It's where we find the impossible possible and surprise ourselves by the strength of our conviction and the courage we can muster to see them through.

The old adage suggests that we should do a little bit of something that scares us every day. By embracing courage and bravery as a life skill, rather than a tool for emergencies only, we learn to flex the bravery muscle and expand our capability and potential. And, the more we do it, the easier and less intimidating it becomes.

Anything that scares you requires courage and bravery to action. Start with small things that push you out your comfort zone for a few minutes. The more you embrace the challenge zone as a playground for your own development, the braver you will get and the easier courage will be to muster when you need it.

Everyone has a different size comfort zone, some are wider than others. Going to an interview isn't something you may require courage for, but Elaine did. We are all different, we are scared of different things and require courage and bravery for a whole host of situations and events that may be second nature to others. What's important is that you recognise your comfort zone and actively push yourself into the challenge zone, so you can gain greater, quicker access to these crucial tools. Remember, being scared is okay and normal – watch the drama rating that you apply to "being scared" or what you are fearful of (see Chapter 7) and make sure this isn't over the top.

Power Up: Change Your Physiology and Self-Talk

We need to be brave when we are scared of something. The problem is that fear is around every corner. Being scared is normal. It's a natural response designed to keep us safe and stop us from doing stuff that might hurt us. It's just biology – the fight, flight or freeze response we've mentioned before.

What's really cool is that we can influence what hormones are released and therefore how we feel just by powering up and changing our physiology and self-talk.

In her TED Talk, social psychologist Amy Cuddy explains a 2-minute "life hack" for improving our chances of a scary or high pressure situation going well – simply by engaging in what she calls a "power pose" before the event or situation. There are several power poses to choose from including standing like a super-hero with your legs hip distance apart and your hands on your hips or sitting with your feet up on a desk and your hands clasped behind your head. All high-power poses increase the physical space we take up with our body. Low-power poses achieve the opposite, so that we shrink the physical space we occupy, such as hunching our shoulders, or holding our arms close to our body, so we make ourselves smaller.

Cuddy and her main collaborator, Dana Carney, from Berkeley, wanted to know, "Can you fake it till you make it?" In other words, can we fake confidence or bravery until we actually feel it? To test the theory a group of volunteers were asked to spit into a vial, so that their baseline levels of testosterone (confidence hormone) and cortisol (stress hormone) could be measured. Half the participants were then told to engage in high power poses and the other half engaged in low power poses although neither group were told which were which, or the purpose of the experiment, so they couldn't guess the nature of the poses. After just two minutes each participant's hormone levels were re-tested. What was astonishing was that two minutes of physical posturing was enough to change their physiology. The high-power pose group experienced a 20 per cent increase in testosterone and a 25 per cent reduction of cortisol, whereas the low power pose group experienced a 10 per cent decrease in testosterone and a 15 per cent increase in cortisol levels.

If we are to access our bravery we need also to access our confidence and positivity, to be assured that the risk will be worth it, whilst also minimising the stress we may feel at facing our fears. It makes sense, therefore, to engage in 2 minutes of high-power posing whenever we need a little extra boost.

Self-Talk and Language

Consider what you are thinking about and telling yourself about the situation you face. It's amazing how our brain can turn a relatively straightforward situation into a national emergency or something out of a Martin Scorsese movie (remember Chapter 7 and the drama scale).

Be mindful of the vocabulary you are using. Avoid universal or negative language such as, "I could never … it's not my thing … I'm not good enough … I've never done it before…" etc. So what? As kids, we did new stuff almost every day and thought nothing of it. Steer clear of negative future talk. We can be our worst self limiter.

Ask yourself what the real risks are. Be honest and logical! Could your action lead to death? Unlikely. Are you going to lose a limb or a loved one? Probably not. Chances are you risk looking a little foolish, maybe, or you may experience hurt pride or a dented ego, but these things are not terminal. Your choice may risk a little money or time, but weigh up the pros and cons and take considered action.

Words are powerful and can help you put on a "brave suit", so that even if you don't feel it you can "power up" to get mentally and physically ready.

Accessing Your "Brave Suit"

Most of us can recall times in our life where we have already demonstrated bravery. Perhaps we decided to sky-dive for charity, or to ask someone we liked out for dinner, or intervened in an argument to prevent someone being bullied. Whatever the situation, really reflect on those times and recognise your bravery. It didn't just happen by accident – you created that state of bravery.

Think about what you felt and experienced at the time. Were you upset at how someone was being treated? Were you determined or was it stubbornness that was driving you? Were you being competitive or indignant? Really engage with that experience again so you can familiarise yourself with the resources and feelings that triggered your bravery. Once identified, the combination of emotions and feelings you experienced in the past can be used again to create a sort of "bravery cape" that you can then decide to put on at any time.

This is your bravery superhero persona. Whenever you need to be brave you simply grab your bravery suit to help you navigate through a difficult or scary situation.

Remember, the body and mind are robust. They are built to withstand the good, the bad and the ugly. Some people are propelled into situations they would never willingly get into if they had the choice. Those who discover they have cancer or must face redundancy or the loss of a parent or close relative, for example. Your body and mind naturally adapt so they can deal with adversity. Those who come through times of deep personal tragedy and trauma often look back with surprise at how they made it through – but they did. We all have these reserves. Human beings are remarkable. We are all capable of survival and regeneration, especially when the chips are down.

Beware of getting in your own way. When it comes to fear, you are your own worst enemy and can become a master of excuses (not now, maybe next time...) and reasons why not (I would do it if only my back wasn't aching...). False indignation can also spring from nowhere (I don't want to and no one is going to force me to do something I don't want to do ... so there!). Like most of us, I'm sure you can be pretty impressive when you get on a roll of why you can't, won't, don't want to, or "can't be bothered"! Recognise this is a normal response to fear – it doesn't mean you have to listen to it. Think about what it would really take for you to do something different or challenging and start removing the obstacles – real or perceived!

NLP Mind to Muscle Exercise

This is a fantastic technique created by Michael Hall which I've shortened here. It starts with a principle (i.e. being brave or courageous, for example) or idea and brings it down from the brain to the body (muscle). It's a process that allows you to pull your ideas, beliefs, understanding and inspirations from your mind through to your body by way of actions and behaviours. As with everything practice is key.

Note: Some of these actions might seem a bit odd and you may feel a little silly doing them at first. Just think of it as an opportunity to leave your comfort zone and push into your challenge zone. Go somewhere where you won't be disturbed and try it – it works!

1. **Identify a desired principle (let's take bravery as an example)**

   - What do you know or understand or believe about being brave that you want to set as a frame in your mind? (*An example might be, "I need to be confident and open" or "I'm going to find my inner courage."*)
   - What idea inspires you and what would you like to "feel" in your body and become a program for your way of being in the world? (*An example might be, "I would like to feel robust, courageous or invincible or powerful." Or even, "I might get scared, but it doesn't matter because I can do it anyway"*)

2. **Describe the principle as a belief**

- Stand up and step forward opening your arms high and wide with a big arm gesture while stating your principle as a belief such as, "I believe that I am brave."
- If you need to step forward and say it again with more physical gesturing and a strong tone of voice, do it (you should sound believable to others and yourself!) It's okay to shout and wave your arms about!

3. **Reformat the belief as a decision**

Once the belief is stated in a way that sounds powerful, convincing and is expressed very succinctly so that it feels compelling, reformulate the personal belief so that it takes the form of a personal decision. This personal decision could be anything. For this example, I will use, "Being brave enough to go on holiday on my own."

To do this you need to express your decision:

- Take another step forward with arm gestures and in a strong tone of voice say, "I believe I am brave and I've decided to go on holiday on my own."

4. **Rephrase the belief-decision as a state or experience**

When you fully experience your concept–>belief–>decision as an emotional state, what will you experience? How will you feel?

- Take another step forward with arm gestures and say, "When I believe and decide to be brave I feel (or experience) … (this could be different for different people, examples might be, *I feel empowered, excited, confident, unstoppable…*" – whatever comes to mind about how you feel. You can have more than one word or phrase.

5. **State the actions that you will take as an expression of this concept**

- Take another step forward with arm gestures and say, "The first thing I am going to do today is book a holiday on my own." Doing this will enable you to begin to formulate specific actions that will enable you to execute your principles.
- So, what one thing will you do today to make this happen?
- You will do that? Really? What else will you do?

In summary, all phrases are spoken while standing up and stepping forward, in order, and with a strong, convincing tone of voice and large arm gestures (all these are important even if it looks a bit odd!)

- "I believe……"
- "I believe and I decide to ………"
- "When I believe and decide that I am xxx I feel ………."
- "The first thing I am going to do about it is …………."

You can go through these steps as often as you need to firmly link your mind to muscle. You should notice how it can transform everything even more and creates an even greater sense of empowerment. Only use definite vocabulary (do not use "think" or "might" or any proposal language).

Finally, my last tip comes from Frasier, my 6-year old ski lift buddy. I asked him, "How do you know when you are scared?" Again, Fraser thought about it for a moment and said, "It's when I get that really bad feeling sometimes, so I sing a song to make myself feel better.

Great advice. When you're scared, sing a song, be brave and do it anyway.

> *To believe yourself to be brave is to be brave,*
> *it is the only essential thing.*
>
> –Mark Twain

Additional Resources

Watch: My Facebook clip on Being Brave as a quick refresher of what's in the chapter and extra encouragement when you need to muster some courage.

Watch: *Amy Cuddy's TED Talk* – a great reminder of how important body language is for changing how others see us and how we feel about ourselves.

Read: *Brave Enough: A Mini Instruction Manual for the Soul* by Cheryl Strayed

Read: *Feel The Fear And Do It Anyway: How to Turn Your Fear and Indecision into Confidence and Action* by Susan Jeffers

Chapter 12
Accessing Motivation and Commitment

It was character that got us out of bed,
commitment that moved us into action,
and discipline that enabled us to follow through.

–Zig Ziglar

Do you ever feel absolutely sure that you want to do something, only to find that desire slowly drain away? Have you ever been confused by your own levels of motivation – one day you're "off-the-charts", ready for anything, and the next you can barely drag yourself out of bed? Have you ever beat yourself up about that difference? If so, welcome to the human race! If you've ever wondered if it's even possible to take more active control over your motivation so you can commit to the changes you need to make and muster the motivation to see them through, then this chapter is for you.

We hear about motivation all the time. Have you ever been motivated to join the gym after pigging out over Christmas or Thanksgiving, or thought about giving "get fit" another crack on the New Year's resolution list? Brands use motivation in their straplines and slogans, because motivation is so often touted as the magic bullet that everyone is looking for. Whether it's trying to lose weight, stop smoking, become healthier – you name it – wherever something needs "willpower" motivation is going to be needed and it's hard!

If you are determined to live your life your way, then it's essential that you understand what's going to try to derail you, what speed humps to expect, and how to navigate those potholes to stay on track. And, ironically, it's not really about motivation, it's about commitment. Commitment is key.

Have you ever wondered what the difference is between motivation and commitment? Why does motivation never seem to appear when you need it the most? Simple. Because motivation is a feeling-based emotion. Dr Steve Peters who wrote, *The Chimp Paradox*, believes that in the same way that you can't decide to "be sad" or "be happy" and instantly expect to flick a switch into those emotional states, you can't just decide to "be motivated". Don't get me wrong, you can use your mind and body to alter your physiology to create sadness or happiness or motivation, but it's not an "on/off" phenomenon. If you want to be sad, for example, you can simply look down, hunch your shoulders forward, take small breaths and think of sad things in your life. Given a little time that will change the chemical composition of your internal system as various hormones are released which will bring about a sense of sadness. Happiness is often the opposite – if you open your body up, breathe deeply and look upward, while moving your body through physical exercise and turning your attention to positive experiences then your body will release a different cocktail of chemicals, which will bring about a sense of wellbeing. It's the same with motivation – it's an emotion, so it ebbs and flows just like any other emotion.

Another useful aspect of motivation is appreciating whether you are motivated away from pain or towards pleasure. Based on our personality, outlook and circumstances we will often favour one over the other. Some of us are more motivated away from something that is causing us distress or upset, while others are drawn towards a positive picture of what our lives could be like. This is an important distinction and can often explain why motivation seems to dry up or disappear. Say, for example, you are more naturally motivated away from pain and you are overweight. You go to put on your favourite pair of jeans and can't get the zip fastened. That's it! You've had enough, so you are suddenly motivated to lose the weight and get back into the jeans. The embarrassment of not being able to fit into your clothes is enough pain to trigger the action. But as soon as you lose enough weight to get back in the jeans, the pain is gone and you stop paying attention to what you are eating and wind back the activity. Needless to say, it's not long before you can't fit into those jeans again. When we are motivated away from pain we can often create cycles of motivation and action that takes us out of pain, but then we stop and repeat the whole cycle again a few months later. This can be very frustrating. Being motivated towards pleasure is a much more sustainable type of motivation, especially if you keep moving the goal posts a little so that the positive picture of yourself and your life is always a little ahead of you. Both are useful and we can learn to use both on our journey towards the life we want to live.

Commitment is different from motivation because it is the agreement we make with ourselves about what we want to achieve. Think of commitment like the engine in the car and motivation as the fuel that moves that car from A to B. Put in this context, it's easy to see why some of us simply run out of fuel. We are in the wrong car! Making a clear and conscious commitment to what you actually want in your life is crucial. Too often we make wishy-washy commitments to stuff that we are not really, genuinely committed to. Those outcomes may sound good or look good, but they don't really tap into a bigger, more meaningful "why". Discovering what that outcome is and knowing our "why" is the key to commitment and when we do, the motivation is straightforward. We can access that well-spring of emotion when we need it.

Those who have a "why" to live, can bear with almost any "how".

–**Viktor E. Frankl**

If you aren't *really* committed to something or you don't want it badly enough, and don't appreciate the "why" behind that commitment, then you will always struggle to be successful.

If you don't fully engage with your "why" and appreciate the important outcomes in your life, or have simply committed to something that isn't actually that important to you, then when things get a little tough it will be much too easy to take the easy option or procrastinate. Commitment to something or someone drives your motivation, which is why when you see athletes or Olympians who train for hours a day for weeks and years, they are utterly committed to their cause/goal/dream. It is THAT desire to stand on the podium that gets them out of bed early, come rain, hail or shine.

First Steps Toward Change

Whatever you want to achieve you have to first decide how much you want it or want to change something. On a scale of 1–10, with 1 being "I don't care" and 10 being "It must happen", if you aren't over an 8 on your chosen objective then I wouldn't even bother. You will just get frustrated and despondent, which can adversely impact your self-esteem and negatively impact your confidence.

In fact, if you are the type of person who puts off taking action because of previous perceived failures or an inability to follow through, I would strongly suggest that you reflect on those so-called failures. If you really think about your past experiences I would wager that your inability to deliver on those commitments was not because you weren't capable, you just didn't want it enough at that time. Remember, timing is important for people. We can only donate so much time to certain things, which is why this book helps you to get rid of the stuff that takes up brain space, to allow you to work on something that will positively contribute to your life.

Stop committing to sh*t you have no interest in delivering, or for which you can't clearly see the bigger "why" picture. Because if you can't, you won't have the necessary motivation to successfully reach your destination. It's a pointless waste of your time and mental energy. Instead, focus on the stuff that really matters – the 9/10 or 10/10 stuff that you absolutely must make happen.

Tips and Strategies

Desire is the key to motivation, but it's determination and commitment to an unrelenting pursuit of your goal – a commitment to excellence – that will enable you to attain the success you seek.

–Mario Andretti

Motivation will only really kick in and be there consistently when you need it once you've made a real commitment to change and appreciate "why" that change is essential. And that means getting really clear on your goals, the change you wish to implement, or your dreams. Even if the motivation does take the odd dip, it doesn't matter as you will find it again because of your commitment.

You can use the "choice mind map" in Chapter 13 to help you positively decide what you want to create in place of what's currently in your world. Or you can start in the opposite direction. Figure out what you *don't* want and work forwards from there! Remember, the goals, changes or dreams don't have to be big or impressive, and you don't need to tell everyone about them. These are for you and you alone and often when we start with the small things and get rid of a few of the issues that cause us endless hassle, then we can build up our confidence and use this incremental process as stepping stones toward creating our life our way. A good way to figure out whether you want something or not is to close your eyes and imagine that you have it or have achieved it already. What does it feel like? What does it look like? What do you notice about yourself? Imagining yourself already there can be a powerful motivational tool to use.

The following GROW model is one of the simplest and most powerful coaching models I use when working with clients. It helps them to clarify their goal, appreciate where they are now, and understand what they need to do to move toward their goal in an honest and open way.

The GROW Model, created by John Whitmore in 1985, is an acronym standing for:

(G)oals
(R)eality
(O)ptions and
(W)ill

These four stages raise an individual's awareness and understanding of what they want, where they are now, what they could do, and what they WILL do.

GOAL	REALITY	OPTIONS	WILL
Your own aspirations	Your current situation and beliefs	The possibilities and resources open to you	The actions you want to take to achieve your personal and professional goals
What do you want?	Where are you now?	What could you do?	What WILL you do? a.k.a Commitment

So, let's get cracking. If you have something in mind that you want to commit to, and are keen to ensure you have access to the required levels of motivation to see it through, then work through the series of questions below. Be honest with your answers – it will help you to have accountability and to act with authenticity, both of which are key ingredients to success. It will also help you get really clear on your end goal, to make sure that it really is something that you want to make happen. If it turns out that it's not that important to you, then you've saved yourself a lot of time and effort. Remember, life is short. Learning how to use that time and effort towards something that really matters to you is essential.

GOAL/DREAM/DESIRE

1. What is it that you want?
2. If you knew you could not fail, what would you want to

achieve/change?

3. How important is this to you (if it's less than an 8 out of 10 stop now!)

4. What are you passionate about?

5. If you achieved what you want, what would it look like? You can draw pictures, or create a vision board using images from magazines if this helps to clarify and articulate your goal to yourself. I would encourage you to use the headings, "What will it *feel* like?", "What will it *look* like?", "What will I *hear* people say?" etc. Use all your senses to get a full spectrum experience of your goal.

6. What will other people notice about you that is different?

7. What new skills or behaviours will help you achieve it?

REALITY

1. What is getting in the way right now of you achieving your goal or making the change? Think about your current situation…

2. Are there any external challenges or barriers?

3. Are these real or assumed?

4. Are there any internal challenges or barriers?

5. Are these real or assumed?

6. What is really getting in your way? Is it fact, fiction or assumption? Investigate the situation and get rid of the fiction and the assumption.

7. What are the excuses you usually use for not following through or achieving what you set out to achieve?

8. What are you scared of? Come on, be honest! If you name it you can deal with it. Often being honest about this can help you realise just how irrational and ridiculous that fear

really is. Often these fears are throwbacks from when we were kids and they are simply not relevant now.

9. Where are you sabotaging yourself?
10. If you don't pursue this goal or make this change what will you feel like in 5 years? Where will you be? Does that prospect make you happy or miserable? Use that emotion to fuel your commitment.

OPTIONS

1. What could you do first?
2. Who else might support you or help you where you might need it?
3. What resources do you already have? What are you already good at? What physical or financial resources do you already have? What skills or contacts could be helpful to you here?
4. What else could you do? Be creative! Think outside the box. Who could you call on, what could you learn? Do you know anyone else who wants the same thing that you could team up with?
5. And what else?
6. If nothing was getting in your way, what would you be doing or do now?
7. What would be the benefit of doing this, or the consequences of not doing it?

WILL (Commitment)

1. What WILL you do now as a first step?
2. How committed are you now to reaching your goal/desire?

3. If it's not a 10 out of 10, what would it take to get you there?
4. Who do you now need to speak to about your commitment?
5. When will you do it?
6. Is there anything else you need to consider before starting?
7. How are you going to celebrate when you achieve your goal or make the change?

Beware self sabotage, lack of confidence and fear, as they can easily throw you off track. Watch out for these three thieves and be ready for them, expect them. Do not let them get in the way of doing what you want to do. There is always a period of uncertainty and discomfort when we are making changes. The status quo is known – even if it's terrible – there is a comfort in the predictability of that situation. Change is never easy, but it's always worth it. Keep your eye on the prize, acknowledge your fears and trepidation, but remind yourself that you are going to be doing it anyway. Feel the fear and do it anyway!

I know where I'm going and I know the truth,
and I don't have to be what you want me to be.
I'm free to be what I want.

Muhammad Ali

Additional Resources

Watch: *Mindshift* – a short provocative film that reminds you why taking action is important and can benefit you, versus waiting and never seizing the moment.

Read: *The Chimp Paradox: The Mind Management Programme to Help You Achieve Success, Confidence and Happiness* by Dr Steve Peters who explains an incredibly powerful mind management model that can help you become a happy, confident, healthier and more successful person.

Read: *What's Stopping You?: Why Smart People Don't Always Reach Their Potential and How You Can* by Robert Kelsey, who provides a practical guide to attacking the most common of phobias: fear of failure.

Chapter 13
Creating Choice in Your Life

One's philosophy is not best expressed in words; it is expressed in the choices one makes... and the choices we make are ultimately our responsibility.

–**Eleanor Roosevelt**

Do you ever feel that the older you get the fewer choices you have? Are you often overwhelmed by the number of choices you face, or limited by the lack of choices you have? Do you ever feel trapped, unsure whether to go right or left? Are you ever anxious about making the right choice or even identifying what your choices are in any given situation? If so, you are not alone.

We all have choices, but sometimes we think we don't. We tread water in a job we hate or a relationship that is no longer working and we even go to parties we don't want to go to because we don't think we have a choice. We do. We always do. Appreciating that fact is what this chapter is all about.

Quite simply, identifying and making choices is one of the most powerful things we can do to influence the quality of our lives. We may not have control over every aspect of our life, but we always have control over our choices – it's just easy to lose sight of that. Choice gives us freedom, and that's why it's so powerful. Of course, we are all unique, so the choices we make are unique, often influenced by our experiences and where we have come from. But perhaps most importantly of all, our choices shape who we are and ultimately determine where we are going and what we will achieve in life.

Choices are not the same as decisions. Choices are about identifying the various opportunity paths available to us, whereas decisions are about which path we decide to pursue. Clearly they are connected, but too often we don't even really consider all the choices we have and this can lead us to feeling stuck or overwhelmed. Neither feels great.

Taking the time to genuinely identify the various choices open to us also helps free us from unhelpful narrative loops. Often, we get stuck in what we "should" or "could" do and we forget we actually have a choice in whether we do something or not. When I left a very well paid corporate job to work for myself as a consultant, it was initially a very challenging transition. I had worked full-time since I was 18 years old, so not going to an office every day was harder than I expected it would be – especially considering I really wanted to get out of the rat-race. I chose to leave that environment and yet it was still difficult to make the shift from employed to self-employed. Before leaving, I'd secured some consultancy work with my previous company, but I needed to look for additional contracts. Only, I'd never had to secure my own contracts before. I wasn't even sure I could and I experienced a crisis of confidence. My narrative loop consisted of berating myself with, "I really should be doing more" or "I could be more proactive about securing work" weekly, daily and sometimes even hourly! It was completely exhausting and consuming.

Figure 13.1 An illustration of my narrative loop

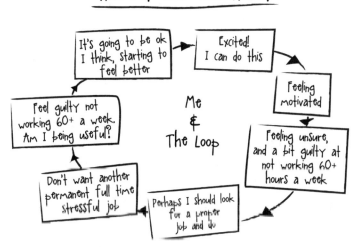

It was also extremely frustrating that I couldn't break out of it, despite being an experienced coach. It took another pair of eyes to help me identify the exit sign. It was simple. After listening to me run through my narrative loop, my friend who is also a senior coach, said, "Paula, I'm hearing you use the words 'should' and 'could' a lot when you talk about this situation. How about you replace those phrases with 'I choose to'?" It was a simple little shift in my vocabulary that stopped my narrative loop. I changed "I should" or "I could" to, "I choose not to work in a permanent job and that's okay … I'm choosing to work for myself and I'm doing okay … I'm choosing to work less hours than I used to because 60 hours a week was unhealthy and stressful and I choose to have a different life..." Since tweaking the language I use to describe my choices, I haven't even thought about it again. Often the quality of our life is not just about identifying new choices, it is also about taking control of the choices we have already made! Re-framing our choices to position them in a new, positive and more constructive light can make a huge difference and free us from being a victim to the outcome or narrative loop.

We make choices all the time, from whether we want tea or coffee, to what we will wear to work, to what we're having for dinner. Most of these choices are easy and quick to make. Sometimes the right choice is obvious, often it's not. Occasionally, we will simply stick our heads in the sand and resist making choices at all. This often comes down to a culmination of stress, or an institutionalised situation where we've lived with something so long we've lost all hope of an alternative reality. Ironically, it's often when we really need new ideas and options that our creativity and ability to muster those options seems to desert us. Of course, when this happens it can be very easy to find other people who are more than willing to make the choice for us. In fact, you need to be vigilant, because other people may try and make your choices for you, even when you have a clear idea of what you want.

Figure 13.2: Being Railroaded by Others

⚠

Beware of other people closing down your options or diminishing your possible choices before you have had time to fully explore them for yourself. Remember, other people's advice is usually simply a reflection of what they would do (or not do) in the situation, often based on their past experience, not yours. Their insight may not be what's best for you. Although it's always wise to seek advice and gather more information, just remember that everyone has their own boundaries, experiences and risk tolerance. Take what makes sense to you and gives you fresh ideas and leave the rest. Don't tie any emotion or judgement to those opinions.

The First Step Toward Change

First, it's important to know that you always have a choice. You may not have thought of them all, or they may not be very appealing, but different options always exist. Identifying your choices doesn't mean you are going to act on them all. Use that insight to free your thinking and reach for what you really want and where you really want to be in your life.

Here are some ideas to help you get started:

- **Check the words you are using to describe your choices** (or lack of them). If you are using words like "I should", "I have to" or "I could" you are giving yourself no room to manoeuvre. Consider changing your language to "I chose to … and I'm OK with that."

- **Keep things simple**, don't over complicate the situation. Seek to separate the facts from the emotion, assumptions or unsubstantiated opinion.
- When exploring your choices **don't run too far ahead in your mind**. Stick to what you know right now and what you can reasonably assume about the consequences.
- **Beware of searching for instant gratification** – think of the bigger picture. Sometimes we have to make tough choices now for a better future tomorrow.
- **Think of at least five choices you could make in this situation**, from the most uncomfortable to the most ridiculous. Include what you would never do, push yourself to be creative without necessarily thinking about a final outcome for any of the options.
- **Think about what *you* really enjoy**, want and would like to achieve. At this point it's about you not others.
- **Which choice takes you closer to your desired outcome?** Which takes you further away?
- **What will contribute towards your happiness along the way?** Take steps to build some of these things into your life as you make the transition, so you can enjoy little "wins" as you move forward – especially if you need to make a tough choice.

It's important to create the right environment so you can focus on some quality thinking time. The calmer your surroundings and the more space you give yourself to fully consider your choices the better. Not only does the peace and quiet allow you to pull in additional information and come up with creative thoughts, it also helps to ignite your intuition or gut response to the choices you come up with. If you give yourself the gift of some quiet time and are able to clearly articulate your choices, you will often experience a physical reaction to the one that "just feels right". This is important to pay attention to because it helps to balance out your "thinking brain".

Tips and Strategies

> *Take care to get what you like or*
> *you will be forced to like what you get.*
>
> **–George Bernard Shaw**

Being confused or unsure is never fun. It can be draining to turn something over and over in your mind, never quite sure what path to take for the best. The following strategies can help you to make progress, so you can identify the choices available to you and make the best one for you at the time.

Create a Choice Mind Map

A very useful exercise to help you create some choices is to create a "choice mind map" for yourself, exhaust each path, good and bad, and articulate the fear or joy. Force yourself to think of at least four or five possible choices to start with – no matter how crazy or unlikely!

Let's take the classic example of a career choice. Say, you hate your job but you've been doing the same thing for such a long time that you are unsure if you are qualified to, or could actually do anything else. You feel it would be impossible to move to something different, you lack the confidence to even try, and are unsure what other choices you have.

Figure 13.3: Illustration of a Choice Mind Map

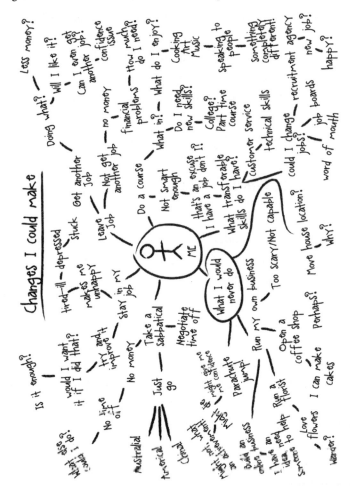

This process will help you to identify new choice paths that you may not have even thought about yet. Creating this map and putting pen to paper also helps to trigger new ideas that may surprise you! Not all the choices you come up with will be viable or even sensible, but this process will enable you to think bigger, test some assumptions and think outside the box. You never know, the answer could be staring right back at you. It may even be making you feel a little uncomfortable, in a good way!

Look for leverage points – more than one or two reasons to pursue a certain choice. This helps to gather weight and momentum behind one favoured option. These kinds of maps can also help you link things together in a way that make what you want to achieve seem more possible.

Help with Hard Choices

I have no choice about whether or not I have Parkinsons. I have nothing but choices about how I react to it. In those choices, there's freedom to do a lot of things in areas that I wouldn't have otherwise found myself in.

–Michael J. Fox

As an adult, we are all faced with tough choices from time to time. It's a normal part of the world we live in. Quite often they come about when none of the choices we have deliver a benefit or "upside". When there is a clear winner, or the choice is a simple one with few ramifications, it is often easy and we move on quickly. But what do we do if there is no clear winner? What if the ramifications are serious? And, what do we do if all the options appear negative or difficult? All we can do is seek to come up with better options based on what we know, what we believe and, just as importantly, what we feel. To give you some extra guidance these ideas have always been helpful to me:

- **Consider the bigger picture**. Does the choice ensure a longer-term benefit? If you can see a benefit, even if it's going to take a while to come to fruition, it will be easier to make that tough choice.

- **Seek to make your choice with the best intentions and interests of others and yourself.** Remember, even seemingly selfish choices can be made with the best intentions for all involved.

- **If your choices are likely to impact others negatively, think about what you can do to support or mitigate that impact**. Hard choices are often hard because we have to communicate those choices with those we care about, who may or may not understand the reasons. If you can help them to understand, then do so, but all that really matters is that *you* understand your reasons. Your reasons are good enough.

- **Don't act on emotional impulse.** Emotions can easily cloud your judgement and whilst we may be impacted by certain emotions or situations, the clearer you can be when making choices the better they will be. Sleep on them. Let your emotions subside before committing to your choice.

- **Use a mentor or coach to help you identify and navigate the choices you face**. A mentor can help you think of things you may not have considered, can bring an invaluable new perspective and support you during the process.

- **Ask the advice of those you admire or respect**. Perhaps surprisingly, these individuals can be alive or dead. Imagine they are in your corner and are looking out for you. What would they say to you and how would they support you through any choices you may need to make? (see Three Mentors process in Chapter 10).

- **Stay open and flexible to alterations.** We don't make

choices and then just sit back and forget about them. We shape them, we grow them and, most of the time, work hard to make sure they are successful. And remember, the downside is rarely as bad as you think it might be.

- **We are a product of our choices. Embrace that!** The benefit of making different choices is that they can take us down paths we may never have experienced before (good and bad). It is these adventures that shape us into the people we are.

- **Use the breathing technique in Chapter 7 to help you get calm** and in a place where you can empty your mind and get creative and open to ideas. It's really hard to be creative with choices if your mind is full of stress and anxiety.

And finally, making choices is just about identifying options until you decide to take action. So be creative, feel your way through the choices you face. Usually a natural winner will emerge if you just give yourself some space to appreciate it. Then you need courage to see it through.

> *It takes courage*
> *To do what you want*
> *Other people*
> *Have a lot of plans for you*
> *Nobody wants you to do*
> *What you want to do*
> *They want you to go on their trip*
> *But you can do what you want*

-Joseph Campbell

Additional Resources

Watch: My Facebook clip on Choices – a useful visual recap of the chapter.

Watch: *Ruth Chang's Ted Talk on How to make Hard Choices* and whether the choices you have in front of you are those you think are equal, are actually equal, or are not equal. When faced with choices we need to make we can often feel stuck. Re-read Chapter 1: Reality Check, for more ideas.

Read: *Mindset: How We Can Learn to Fulfil Our Potential* by Carol Dweck who looks at the "Growth" and "Fixed" mind-sets and how they influence what we think is possible for us and the choices that are therefore open to us.

Chapter 14
How to Make Big or Difficult Decisions

An expert is someone who has succeeded in making decisions and judgements simpler through knowing what to pay attention to and what to ignore.

–**Edward de Bono**

Are you struggling to make a big, difficult or important decision? Or do you know that you are going to have to make that type of decision soon? Are you unsure what the right course of action is? Does the size of the choice seem too daunting? Do you feel paralysed as you wrestle on the horns of a dilemma? Are you just really bad at making decisions? Do you feel that you often make the wrong call? If so, then this chapter may offer some suggestions to help.

Life is full of decisions, most of them small or daily decisions, such as what to eat for lunch and what to wear to work. Others are bigger because they have bigger or more far-reaching consequences, which make them harder to make. These hard decisions can cause stress, anxiety and worry and our brain can very easily get trapped in a loop – playing various scenarios over and over again in a bid to try and work out what to do.

First Steps Toward Change

Give yourself some time…

When I got married to my now husband he and I lived in two different parts of the country, exactly 120 miles apart. Although we both worked in London, we both had families in our respective parts of the country. It became very clear that if we were to be together then we would have to make a decision about where we were going to live. Some sort of move was essential to solve the distance issue. But this was a big decision for both of us for lots of different reasons. So big that we commuted between the two places for the first couple of years. It was a slog driving back and forth each week, but it solved the immediate problem, even though we both recognised it wasn't a permanent solution.

I was concerned about moving to where my husband lived because it was far away from my family and friends and I was anxious about losing my support networks. I also wasn't sure

I'd like the area. Of course, we had two houses, so one really needed to be sold and mine was the obvious candidate, but I wasn't sure if we should buy or rent in the new location – wherever we decided that to be. The decision was finally sped up when I left my job in London to be a consultant, so my physical location wasn't quite as important anymore, plus my youngest son went off to university. We really needed to make a decision and this did add to our stress levels. I was definitely in my comfort zone where I was, as I'd lived there for 16 years. Fortunately, I was able to use a number of strategies I've outlined in this chapter and others (including pushing into the Challenge Zone described in Chapter 11) to help me. We moved permanently to my husband's location and I absolutely love it.

This decision was so difficult for us both because it wasn't just about us. Our choice was going to impact other people – friends and family – and that definitely made the decision harder.

When making tough decisions, everyone seems to have advice, whether we ask for that advice or not. Some decisions can be unpopular with other people, especially loved ones, so we internalise those decisions and stew over them ourselves. It can cause sleepless nights and create an overbearing negative mood as we feel pressured to do the right thing. But it's also worth remembering that making big decisions can also be exciting and liberating as we consciously and purposely open up to a wonderful world of opportunity in our lives. For the most part, we normally make decisions based on something that will improve or better our lives, situation or family. No one sets out wanting to make a bad decision, so make sure you are doing it for the right reasons – i.e. for you and people you care about.

Tips and Strategies

Nothing is more difficult, and therefore more precious,
than to be able to decide.

–Napoleon Bonaparte

Below are some tips and strategies you can use to help you make the tough choices we all have to make from time to time.

Create Appropriate Decision Lists

In an effort to clarify what we need to think about and what we need to make decisions on, many of us will make a list. This list, either written or mental, may include things like:

- What am I going to make for dinner?
- What colour dress shall I wear on Saturday night?
- Shall I phone my mother tonight or at the weekend?
- Shall I paint the downstairs loo blue or green?
- Should I resign from work so I can change career and buy a coffee shop?
- Am I going to watch *Game of Thrones* or *Masterchef* tonight?
- Do I want to go on holiday to Spain or Italy?

You will probably have already realised that "resign from work so I can change career and buy a coffee shop" really doesn't belong in that list. It's not a quick 2-second or even 1-minute decision, and yet it's sitting in the same "decision list" in our mind. Our brain is a wonderful tool; it can be very efficient when putting all the decisions we need to make in one place, but it's not great at separating the small decisions from the big ones – unless directed.

When it comes to decisions, the small or quick decisions are usually naturally separated from the big, laborious ones because of consequences. What am I going to make for dinner is much easier to answer because it has far fewer consequences than whether or not I should resign. Make the "wrong" choice on dinner and I smell of garlic bread all night or suffer a mild case of indigestion. Make the "wrong" choice on whether to resign or not and I could experience serious financial problems!

There is however also a "head space" issue to wrestle with. We might imagine that it's only the big decisions that take up head space, but that isn't necessarily the case. I may need to decide about whether I'm going to resign or not, but I also have an important function in two weeks and need to decide what to wear and I need to clear the air with a friend. The last two issues arguably have fewer consequences than the first, but it doesn't stop them sapping energy and taking up headspace.

When different types of decisions are on the same list, even if it's just a mental list, the inconsistency of those decisions can interfere with our decision-making ability. This can easily become exhausting and repetitive. Either we don't clear some of the easy decisions which can give us more head space and energy to really consider the big issues, or we constantly skip past the big ones in "too busy" mode – which means we repeatedly avoid the ones that have major consequences for our on-going health and happiness. If that happens, even adding a few decisions we've already made, just so we can tick them off, won't help to make us feel better. The challenge, for most of us anyway, is we already know that the only way to really feel better is to grasp the nettle and make the important decisions – regardless of how big or small they may be.

Below are some tips and strategies to help you differentiate between types of decision, make appropriate decision lists and work through them all, including the big decisions:

- **Your first action is to consider whether there is actually a decision to make**. Is it possible that you've simply fooled yourself into thinking there is a decision to make? Ask yourself, "Is there actually a decision to be made AT ALL?" An example might be, my mother/father are getting older and they need to think about selling their house as they won't be able to cope on their own. Should I have them move in with me? I should, because I am their only child and they looked after me. Hmm, is my house big enough? What would I need to do? Would they like it? Would we like living together? Etc, etc. They might not be in a position where they can't look after themselves for another two, three or more years, but sometimes we can *pull forward* decision making before we actually need to. There is nothing wrong with planning ahead, but make sure you're not forcing yourself into some kind of action that doesn't need to happen. In any case, the situation could change and you may have wasted days, weeks, months worrying about it!

- **What's the timing on the decision?** Does it really need to be made today, or will next week, next month or next year be quick enough? If the decision is not urgent then take some of the angst out of the decision by adding a timeline. Again, if a decision is sitting in your daily or more mundane decision list, it can take on an unnecessary sense of urgency or importance that it really doesn't warrant. Conversely, be mindful not to put off key decisions and pretend that you have more time than you actually do. If you can't make the decision, decide when you will make it and give yourself some time.

- **Remember, big decisions can sometimes disappear if events or circumstances change.** Or the decision can become less important or relevant. Remember to move it from your list or re-prioritise if it does.

- **Moving the bigger decisions into a category all on their own is helpful.** If I know I want to dedicate some time to the decision process I might do research, ask people's advice, etc. Taking yourself off somewhere quiet to think, outside, with fresh air is good. You can't possibly make time for thinking when you are in the humdrum of work or in a noisy home.

- **Accept that big decisions with far-reaching consequences are going to upset your daily rhythm.** This is actually one of the reasons they are so tough to make. We are essentially creatures of habit, and decisions that could potentially disrupt that routine or turn our lives upside down are naturally tougher to make. If those are the type of decisions you need to make, you are going to have to prepare yourself for some fallout.

- **Adding pros and cons to your decisions** can be really useful to help you gain clarity around the advantages and disadvantages of your decision. Just make sure you do it without filters or bias and you are balancing positive AND negative statements. If you are doing this with a family member or partner it's good to come up with a list separately, as you won't then influence each other during the process.

- **Consider ordering the pros and cons from most important to least important** or adding a weighting system to them. It's usually not as simple as adding up the pros and cons of each. If a pro is significant enough, it can quite easily cancel out several cons and vice versa.

- **Just because it's a "no-brainer" doesn't make it right.** Sometimes decisions, including tough decisions, can seem really obvious or logical – a "no-brainer". They might make financial sense, logistical sense, be a wonderful opportunity etc, but that doesn't automatically mean it's the right decision for you. If you feel some reservations – pay attention to those feelings.

  - Check the "fear factor". Fear is normal when we make changes or there is a big decision that we want to make where the future or outcome is unknown. Don't confuse "fear" with the fact that it might not "feel right". Identify the fear and articulate it, then re-assess the feeling to help guide your decision making.

- **Watch out for 3rd party advice** – some people might not like your potential decision or feel uncomfortable with it because they are not brave enough or would never make that type of decision. They may have a vested interest in the status quo and therefore seek to put you off by predicting doom and gloom. By all means investigate the sensible suggestions, but don't get unnecessarily side tracked from your choice.

- **Watch out for spontaneity and impulse.** If this is in your character it can be your friend and your enemy. I went out to buy a loaf of bread once and ended up buying a car instead (true story). Whilst this can feel invigorating, as though we are powering through decisions, it can also lead to problems if the decision is made too quickly or without enough rigour. If you are prone to falling in love with ideas rather than assessing the reality of them, do your research and ask someone's advice that you trust!

Beware! **Watch out for making decisions that please other people and not you. We can be heavily persuaded sometimes to make decisions that may not be right for us. You will know because you will feel it – somewhere in your body. Pay attention to this and make sure you discuss it. You feel that way for a reason. Explore it before you say yes. It may come back to haunt you later if you don't.**

Run the Decision Through Your Mind–Body System

It's important to run your decision making through your whole "body and mind system". This prevents your brain from "out-thinking" you or "overthinking" for you. Use the following NLP technique to run a decision through your mind-body system:

- Take yourself off to somewhere quiet and close your eyes.
- Practice the breathing technique from Chapter 4 to relax your mind and connect yourself to your body.
- Calm your brain. It should be empty of thoughts and all you should be doing is breathing peacefully and calmly.
- Once you feel relaxed and peaceful, step through the decision you would like to make (there might be more than one that you want to run through, but do them one at a time).
- Imagine yourself making the decision and what your world will look like once you have made it. Think with detail – what happens that day after you make it? Where do you go, what do you do, what do other people do? Are people happy or sad? Do you feel happy or sad? Does your heart feel joy and happiness or are you feeling an uneasiness? If fear starts to emerge, remind yourself you are safe to make this decision right now, in this safe space of breathing and calm. Decide to remove or ignore the fear and concentrate on how it feels once the decision has been made. Do you feel mainly positive or negative feelings? Use these insights to guide you.
- Remember to keep calmly breathing. All is well with the world.
- You can do this a couple of times with a different outcome if that's helpful to you.
- After this process, you will get a better idea of how your body feels in relation to this decision and whether it feels "right".
- Remember, timing can play a part here. Just because it doesn't feel right, right now, may just mean it's not the right time for the decision. Try it again at a later date and see whether it feels different.

Toss a Coin

Another really simple and easy way to run your decision through your mind-body system is to toss a coin! This may sound really superficial, but tossing a coin can actually be really useful – but not in the way you might imagine. Say you are struggling to make a choice between two options, A and B.

By assigning each option to "heads" or "tails" you get an opportunity to quickly access your mind-body system or "gut response". Say, for example, you don't know whether you should resign from your job or stay in the role. You decide that you are going to toss a coin to decide and assign "heads" to resign and "tails" to stay. You toss the coin, catch it and slap it onto the back of your hand, slowly removing your hand to reveal your destiny! The second you see the result you will have a reaction. Pay attention to that reaction. Were you disappointed? Were you upset? Were you thrilled?

The idea of the coin toss is not to put your fate at the mercy of chance, but to reveal what "feels right" for you, or to expose the option that on some level you do want to pursue, even if you are not fully conscious of it. Decisions are not just logical and cognitive, they are physical. We hear people say all the time, "Oh, I don't know why I chose that, it just *felt* right." Tossing a coin allows you to circumvent the mind to quickly access your instinct about what's the right choice for you.

How to Stop Repeating Bad Decisions

We've all made some bad decisions in our lives. The key is to learn from them and make sure we don't repeat them over and over again. Our life is full of paths that we take. Some are wrong turns and detours. The trick is being able to identify those as quickly as possible so you can get back on the path that will take you where you want to go. If you have a tendency to repeat the same poor decisions (or keep taking the same dodgy shortcut that ends up getting you in trouble) and would like some help to break this unhelpful pattern, here are some things to think about:

- **Familiar and comfortable isn't always good.** Human nature means that we tend to choose what's familiar or comfortable. But if familiar and comfortable always end badly for you then you need a new approach. Remember, Einstein once said, the definition of insanity is doing the same thing over and over again and expecting a different result. There is nothing inherently wrong with familiar and comfortable, but if it's not working you need to challenge your childhood and adult experiences that have created this bias. Our past experiences always influence our current ability to choose, because we attach certain beliefs and expectations to the outcome. These experiences can make us feel like we aren't worthy of better or don't deserve to be happy, so we just take more of what we know, even when it's not what we want. It's time to be brave, try something different, make a different decision and choose a different outcome. Not only will this help to break the negative loop, but it will increase your confidence.

- **Give yourself some breathing space.** If you make decisions when you are stressed or tired or when you feel forced into a corner, you are much more likely to make a poor decision without thinking it through.

- **Appreciate the influence others have.** When committed, other people can easily influence us into doing what *they* want us to do, whilst making it look like they are doing it for our own good! Alternatively, friends and loved ones can make us feel as though they know what's best for us or know more about the situation. Make sure your choices are *your* choices, and not someone else's. Never be persuaded by another person. Go with your gut. Then at least if it fails you can own that error and move forward without blame and recrimination.

- **It's normal to feel uncomfortable and scared.** Appreciate that making a difficult decision, or choosing an unusual or unfamiliar option, will almost always feel a bit scary and uncomfortable. It's okay – it's just different (and exciting if you allow it to be).

- **Beware of your inner voice of "conformity"** – the one that whispers that you "have to", you "should" do something or behave in a certain way. Your choices should be about what "you want to do", not some out-dated expectation of what you deserve or are capable of.

> *The things that come to those who wait may be*
> *the things left by those that got there first*
>
> **–Steven Tyler**

Additional Resources

Watch: My Facebook clip on Making Big Decisions – it recaps what's in this chapter and is a useful refresher when you arrive at "decision time".

Read: *Making Great Decisions* by T. D. Jakes

Read: *Start With Why* by Simon Sinek who explains how knowing your "why" can help the decision-making process.

Chapter 15
How to Have a Tough Conversation

The difficulty with this conversation is that it's
very different from most of the ones I've had of late.
Which, as I explained, have mostly been with trees.

–Douglas Adams

Do you find yourself skirting around a conversation, keen to talk about everything from the weather to what's on TV rather than confront the elephant in the room? Do you know you need to discuss something important or difficult with someone, but find you are constantly putting it off because you don't know where to start or what to say? Perhaps you need to have a tough conversation with a friend, loved one, or employee, but can't seem to make yourself do it? Perhaps you've already tried, made a bit of a mess of it and need to clear the air? If so, this chapter may provide some insight into how to open up communication constructively without the drama.

There are few things in life that can't be solved, or at least improved, by a really good conversation! And yet, when that conversation ventures into territory that may upset the other person or has already upset us we can seek to avoid it with single-minded determination.

The human persona has much to blame for this. We like to be liked and so we seek out opportunities where we can be liked and appreciated and avoid situations where we could be unfavourably judged or actively disliked. This means that we often avoid tough conversations where we have to deliver bad news or express something that we fear the other person may not want to hear. We worry about how the other person will handle the news, whether they will be able to see our point of view and whether it will descend into an all-out slanging match. Most of us don't like or relish confrontation and will do almost anything to avoid it, hoping it will all just go away.

But, sometimes having the tough conversation is the only way through the challenge to clear the air and move on constructively. The other reason for having the "hard conversation" is that it is often beneficial to the other person. We often assume that these tough conversations are going to be a nightmare and we are going to upset the other person, and whilst that may be true, sometimes the conversation can lead to personal insight and transformation.

First Steps Toward Change

It makes sense, therefore, that you first consider whether the conversation is needed or not. This may sound odd, but it's surprising how often we get confused about a tough discussion that's necessary and a tough discussion we want to have because our ego is a little bruised or we just want the last word! When things happen, our natural response is that we need to "talk about it". Self-help books are full of advice on the merits of clearing the air, holding others to account, facing our demons, or how we should "lean in and be the bigger person". Whilst none of these pieces of advice are necessarily wrong, they often miss the first most important step: do you need to have this conversation at all or are you falling into the trap of "I must – that's what people do"?

Consider your intention for the conversation. Is it to "state your case" because you are "right"? Or is it to find out more information so you can both better understand what created this situation or tension, and therefore what can resolve it so you can both move on? Do you genuinely want to improve the situation or do you just want to get something off your chest? Are you just wanting an opportunity to say what you wish you'd said the first time – the answer you've now been rehearsing for the last fortnight? If so, then you may want to consider your motives. What are you trying to achieve with this intervention? If it's not resolution and improvement then the chances are you really don't need to have the conversation at all.

Knowing that there is a tough conversation on your horizon can create discomfort and a low-lying level of stress. Assuming you do believe it's important, then it's time to grasp the nettle and take action. Remember, tough conversations don't always need to be uncomfortable, highly charged or stressful. They also present a genuine opportunity to deepen a connection, better understand a situation or person, and learn from others. Misunderstandings, jumping to the wrong conclusions and making assumptions about a situation can all be quickly and efficiently cleared up with an open and honest discussion. Plus, having the conversation instead of role playing it in your head endlessly will be infinitely more constructive and it will reduce your stress and anxiety considerably.

Here are some tips to help you decide if the conversation is even needed!

- **Consider what kind of outcome you want from this conversation.** Is it to repair, strengthen or resolve a situation or relationship? How much do you really care about the situation or the person? If you don't care enough or it's not important to you, do you really need to have the discussion? Probably not!
- **Check your reason for having the hard conversation**. It is because it made you annoyed or angry and you want to "tell someone off"? If so, it could be your ego that wants the conversation rather than you genuinely wanting to resolve something. Someone might have behaved badly, but telling them off is never going to give you a good outcome. Explaining rather than telling is much more effective.
- **Are you ready to hear the other person's side of the story in the conversation?** It's not just you who's going to speak and they will likely have their own point of view or

perception of what happened and what was said. You have to be ready to listen and hear their side without negatively reacting in the moment. You don't necessarily have to like what is said or agree with it, but you must be willing to listen and "agree to disagree", or at least take it on board and consider the alternative "story".

- A good way to prepare for this is to replay the conversation, but from their perspective. Imagine you are them and stand in their shoes. Imagine what they may have felt listening to you AND if their reactions or words were in response to something you said. This can be an incredibly enlightening and is a smart way to give you more insight and information for your conversation. It may sound odd, but you'll be surprised at how accurate this thought experiment can be and how much additional understanding you can glean from the other person's point of view.

- **Be honest about your story.** Try to keep it factual. You can say how it's made you feel, but don't overcook it (see Drama Rating from Chapter 7). Try not to "spin" your story into what you made it mean or throw in assumptions. Keep it brief and factual where you can.

- **If there is a lot of emotion around the situation or person, it's wise to seek to tone down that emotion *before* the conversation.** Or, if you really want to check if you need the conversation this is a good exercise:

  - Get yourself prepared so that you know how you want the conversation to play out. What is it you want to say? What words are you going to use?

  - Visualise the person in a chair sitting opposite you (you can be standing or sitting, whatever you are most comfortable with)

- Now tell them what you would like to say, how it/they made you feel (annoyed, angry or upset) or the pieces of the conversation which you know might upset them if it's not news they want to hear
- Carry on all the way through until you have finished what you want to say
- This can be an empowering act, and will help give you a better idea of how you sound
- In my coaching sessions, I have done this with clients a number of times and usually a couple of things happen:
  - They feel empowered simply by verbalising the conversation and getting it off their chest. Often this is enough and they no longer feel the need to have the conversation with the person at all. Or,
  - They realise that they sound a little ridiculous, melodramatic or emotional and either decide it wasn't that bad after all or it enables them to turn the emotional content of the message down a notch or two, which always helps the eventual outcome.

Tips and Strategies

People say conversation is a lost art; how often I have wished it were.

–Edward R. Murrow

Assuming you have decided that you really do need to have this conversation and there is a bigger benefit for the discussion to both parties than simply you getting something off your chest or appeasing your hurt ego, then here are some tips that can help you to get a better outcome from the conversation.

- **Make proper time for it.** Don't ring on the hoof or grab someone as they walk by and say, "Oh, by the way, I really wanted to talk to you about..." I call this a "drive-by shooting" because that's exactly what it is – disconcerting and surprising for both parties! The other person isn't expecting it (and often neither are you), so it can come across as hostile, which immediately puts both of you on the back foot and into defence mode. Instead, let the other person know you want to catch up and discuss the issue. Keep it casual and non-threatening. This will allow them to gather their thoughts about it before you speak with them.
- **Keep the conversation fairly short.** No one wants to sit through your War and Peace rant about what went wrong or a blow by blow account of a screw up so they can relive it in HD. Remember, it's not about you winning or being right, it's about gathering information and insight towards a better future outcome and an improved relationship.
- **Apologise for any hurt you have caused.** "Sorry" is one of the most powerful words in the English language. It is also a demonstration of strength not weakness. Some people are really bad at apologising and never do it. Being able to reflect and take responsibility for your part in a situation is one of the most underrated skills you could ever develop. It enables you to manage, understand, and navigate through relationships and life in a much easier and less stressful way. Think about what you could have done differently or better to have improved the situation or made it easier for the other person – even when it's them who has made the error or created the situation – and say so. It will show the other person it's not actually all about them and it will show that you are willing to acknowledge your part and work together to create a better outcome.

- **Be authentic.** Make sure that what you are saying matches your face. In other words, if you are saying something you don't really believe it will show and they won't believe you. If you feel nervous beforehand, say so. We are human and none of us are perfect. Articulating honestly how you feel and showing vulnerability will help you connect authentically to the other person. Of course, if you are blazing angry then the "hairdryer treatment" is not going to help (re-visit Chapter 3 before you have the conversation). Remember to use your calm breathing (and don't hold your breath).

- **Don't beat around the bush or ice the cake with a cherry on the top!** It can get confusing for people if you talk around the subject rather than getting to it and it can make you look and sound inauthentic.

- **Think about how you are coming across with your tone and body language**. Be and look as relaxed as you can. Your tone should be one of curiosity, empathy and understanding. Even if it's been a nightmare, if you adopt this approach you will be even more genuine about wanting to bring a resolution.

- **Remember to listen.** You need to show you are hearing them too, so give them time to speak or ask questions – it's a two-way exchange. If you don't agree with something the other person says, you can agree to disagree or you can say, "I'll think about that", so that you don't have to respond immediately.

⚠️

Beware the demanded apology. I've often heard people say to others that they want an apology or they demand an apology. If you have to ask for an apology, then even if you get one it will rarely be sincere, so you won't feel the resolution you desire. If you are demanding an apology, then there is likely an element of control you're looking for, so really think about why that is important. Do you have to hear those *actual words* in order to know someone is sorry? Quite often, if you have the right conversation and they have done something wrong or behaved badly it will come naturally anyway. If it doesn't, look for other signs in their eyes, in their face and demeanour. You might see it without hearing it. Sometimes that is enough.

Finally, not everyone comes to the table ready to solve things. But at least if you try, rather than avoiding it, you will know whether something good can come from the situation. If it doesn't, then at least you know that you tried your best. We don't have 360 degree views on everything and sometimes there is stuff going on for the other person, which means they may not be ready to talk to you or hear what you are saying or be happy about it. That's okay. It's more about them than it is about you, so let it go.

It is more fun to talk with someone who doesn't use long, difficult words but rather short, easy words like "What about lunch?"

–A. A. Milne, Winnie-the-Pooh

Additional Resources

Watch: My Facebook clips on *Having Hard Conversations* part 1 & 2

Read: *Crucial Conversations: Tools for Talking When Stakes Are High* by Patterson, Grenny, McMillan and Switzler for some great insights in this area.

Read: *Difficult Conversations: How to Discuss What Matters Most* by Douglas Stone, Bruce Patton & Sheila Heen – considered a definitive work on handling these unpleasant exchanges and based on 15 years of research at the Harvard Negotiation Project.

Conclusion

So … Have you got your s**t together?

Okay, that's probably an unfair question.

The purpose of this book is to be a practical manual to help you live your life, your way. It's not meant to be a read-once-and-donate-to-the-charity-shop-book. Instead, keep it handy so you can refresh your memory on ideas to help you get through the normal ups and downs of life. It offers tools and techniques that can help you to make the necessary changes, but also to stick with some of the more important things so you can deepen your experiences in that area, rather than constantly jumping out of one frying pan into another fire. Once you have managed to get your s**t together it will mean that you will be in a much better position mentally to help someone else with theirs – and that is a true gift you can give to someone.

Happiness is not a destination, it's the by-product of doing something that is meaningful to you, and learning how to manage those crucial 6 inches between your ears.

But why is it so very important that we learn how to manage ourselves and get our s**t together? Why now?

Well … we are living in extraordinary times.

The speed and scale of change is breath taking, whether it's social, political, technological, environmental, economic or cultural. The things many of us take for granted didn't even exist a few decades ago. Most of us have infinitely more choice and freedom than our parents or grandparents did, and on the face of it that is no bad thing.

But there is a flip side.

I believe these changes are creating a tension between how we are expected to live and behave and how our parents lived and behaved. The "facts" that guided our parent's lives are at best being challenged, and at worse no longer true, accurate or relevant. Each new generation has questioned the previous one, but today the new generation (Gen Y and younger) are increasingly questioning the status quo. They don't believe what they are told, even by accepted voices such as the TV news. We even now have a "fake news" issue that leaves people even more confused as they search for some kind of "truth" in the world. For most, the school system they emerge from is, arguably, useless in preparing them for a world that is changing so rapidly that old style learning is obsolete. We don't need to know everything anymore, and we certainly don't need to know the different names for the various layers of the stratosphere, or who was on the British throne in 1415. We have Google!

On one level this explosion of choice, connectivity, and communication has led to confusion and superficiality – neither of which help us to live deep, rich and meaningful lives. And various research tells us that shallow narcissistic behaviour is becoming a global epidemic. The celebrity "at home with" TV era has told us that we can be famous for doing nothing and contributing nothing, as long as we promote ourselves mercilessly and post endless selfies to social media – ideally semi-naked and pouting! This "dog-eat-dog" competitive selfishness is creating some profoundly unattractive and toxic behaviours in people.

Another consequence of inhabiting a world that's "always on" is that stress and anxiety often become the new "normal". So the pressure to engage with and stay relevant to this changing environment can be exhausting. In an effort to cope, we often either stick our head in the sand and ignore the issues or we micro-manage every last detail of our lives. Neither is a cure. In fact, both options simply amplify the stress and anxiety!

Whether by necessity or design, more and more of us are realising that there really isn't much point having great stuff or a fantastic home if we are killing ourselves working 80 hours a week in two jobs to pay the mortgage and can't even afford to buy a take-out once a month. "Being busy" is one of the 21st Century's most prolific diseases we can succumb to. Time is invaluable. How you spend it really is down to you and only you can manage it, regardless of what you tell yourself, or how you like to define yourself. Time can be and is sometimes traded for money by taking a bigger job, one with more travel, one with more overtime etc., but when is enough money enough? When is having more money worth spending less time with the ones we love? Use your time wisely, once it's gone its gone!

Unfortunately, in our quest for something else, something better or something new, and in our desire to make sweeping changes to our lives, we may throw away more than we need to so we can start again. In fact, this "all or nothing" approach is part of the modern-day malaise.

So, what do we need to know? We need to know how to live with the ups and downs of life more skilfully and create stronger mental resilience. We need to move away from this "all or nothing" mind-set and learn to handle the inevitable twists and turns of life without throwing in the towel when things get a little tough. Or, conversely, staying in terrible situations because of some outmoded belief system or cultural norm.

What we have to appreciate is that the world may be changing rapidly, but the hardware we are using to navigate that world is essentially the same as it's always been. As Nigel Nicholson, professor of Organisational Behaviour at London Business School, once said, "You can take the person out of the Stone Age, but you can't take the Stone Age out of the person." We need to upgrade our operating system so that we can effectively manage this new environment – that's what we need. Being resilient, practical and flexible to what life sends our way is critical in helping us to navigate the seas ahead.

The human mind is extraordinary. Even today we don't fully understand it, but what we do understand can revolutionise our lives. When we finally realise that the quality of our life is directly connected to how we manage that "through traffic" in our brain, and how much control we have over that "airspace", we are liberated by the inevitable struggles of human life. When we appreciate our own strength, resilience and ability to adapt and evolve we can settle into the journey with grace – safe in the knowledge that whatever life throws at us, we will prevail.

Technology is great, but what we really need to navigate this new landscape are real-time strategies and ideas that can help us change the things we need to change without necessarily uprooting our family, divorcing our partner or running off to join the circus. We need new ways to gain much needed perspective "in the moment", so we can develop resilience and emotional intelligence and flexibility that will give us access to more of our best resources and best thinking. This, in turn, will help us to really see our life through new eyes so we can finally differentiate between what really needs changing and what just needs more effort and commitment, or a little nudge in a more constructive direction. We don't always need to change everything all at once, right now. Sometimes we just need to get ourselves in a better frame of mind and live in the "present", so we can see what's really going on instead of being consumed by the stress and drama.

And that's probably the main reason I wrote this book.

Our increasingly throw-away society means it's now culturally acceptable to give up when we are not happy, but that approach will not lead to a deep, rich, meaningful life either. If something sucks in your life then absolutely you need to stop complaining about it and change it. But sometimes, the thing that really needs to change is *us*.

And I know that is easier said than done. And I know that doing some of this stuff requires off-the-scale courage. If, after reading this, you feel a little more empowered, a little braver, and you are now feel more equipped to take whatever that next step might be, then that is bloody fantastic!

Life is precious. Your life is precious. Live it in the way you want to.

You can do it.

I hope this book helps you to do just that.

Acknowledgments

My sincere gratitude goes to Karen McCreadie who has partnered me along this journey, enabling me to write in a way that would make sense to other people outside of my brain. Her practical Scottish wit, humour and smartness has kept me motivated and given me lots of laughs along the way.

I also want to thank my loving husband who has the most reluctant author of a wife. He rugby tackled and pushed me over the line all the way, as well as doing some of the heavy lifting that has made this book a reality!

I also owe thanks to Denise Macrigeanis for helping me navigate my own path, my way, Sue Bayliss, my NLP tutor, and my NLP group of friends who, with journey sharing, support and practicing of techniques, has got me to the place where I have my sh*t together! The NLP techniques in this book are from the great John Grinder and Richard Bandler unless specified.

Contact

Need further help or want to keep updated with ideas and tips? Or just want to get in contact? Well, the connected world has made that 300% easier than it used to be!

Email: paula@paulameir.com
Facebook: Paula Meir
Twitter: @paulameir
YouTube: Paula Meir
Instagram: @paulameir